GREAT FOOD
GLUTEN AND DAIRY FREE
125 Delicious Allergy-Friendly Recipes

PEGGY TREFTS

CONTENTS

INTRODUCTION

MY JOURNEY WITH FOOD CAME ABOUT OUT OF NECESSITY, but quickly turned into a hobby. Before long, I had become a (mostly) real-food advocate and gut-health fanatic.

In 2010, I started suffering with joint pain, swelling, unrelenting fatigue, and weight gain—all of these were new for me. I spent nine months going to doctors of various specialties, just to be told the same thing over and over again: "Yes, something is wrong with you; but I don't know what."

During that time, my general practitioner became interested in a more holistic view of medicine and had been studying up on gut health and the microbiome. She helped me discover that I had severe leaky gut syndrome (a thinning of the small intestinal wall that lets food particles into your blood stream) and *Candida albicans*, an overgrowth of bad yeast in the digestive system. These conditions led to food intolerances and a whole host of health problems!

I eliminated all milk products, eggs, gluten, corn, soy, and refined sugars. After thirty days of a prescription antifungal and a radical diet change, I had lost twenty-three pounds. Joint pain and swelling were gone, and I wasn't tired all the time. In fact, I had more energy than I had had in years!

If you have taken antibiotics or steroids, you are likely to have some form of leaky gut, *Candida albicans*, or food intolerances. But if you take the time to heal your gut and eliminate problem foods, you will feel so much better. Your skin will glow, you will have more energy, and it's quite likely you will lose weight. You might lose a few foods, but you will gain your health!

ABOUT GREAT FOOD GLUTEN AND DAIRY FREE

IN 2012, I STARTED A FOOD BLOG that goes by the name Allergy Free Test Kitchen. It is still up and free for anyone to peruse through the many allergy-free recipes. At the beginning of the blog, I still used sugar, so some of the older recipes no longer fit my philosophy of eating and food preparation.

While there are a *lot* of gluten-free, dairy-free, and allergy-friendly cookbooks out there, I could not find a single one that fit me and my needs. I reviewed a lot of cookbooks for *Gluten Free and More Magazine's* website, My Life with Food Allergies, so I should know! They either called for tons of sugar or too many starches, or they used milk. Many were just poorly written. And you would be surprised how many of the recipes did not work or taste good!

I wanted a cookbook that had great soups, entrees, and sides that everyone could enjoy, even those who do not have celiac disease or gluten sensitivity. I wanted a cookbook with baked goods and treats that were reminiscent of the classics, but without all the sugar. I wanted a cookbook that I could use for years and years. And I wanted a cookbook that could help you feed your food-sensitive friends and families as well as yourself.

The recipes in this book work! I have worked on this book for over four years and tested the recipes endlessly, taking copious notes. My family's meals were often chosen not by what we wanted to eat, but rather by what I was testing for this book. The recipes included are written precisely so even beginner cooks can follow and understand.

These recipes taste great. You could make them for your gluten-eating friends, and they would not even notice or miss the gluten and dairy. These are not the tasteless, dense, and rock-hard, gluten-free, store-bought foods.

But in order for them to work and taste great, you need to make them as written—especially the baked goods and treats. (Be sure to read each chapter introduction, which goes into more detail about the ingredients.) You won't be disappointed. These recipes will be loved by your family for years to come.

STOCKING YOUR KITCHEN

IF YOU ARE MAKING THE SWITCH TO MORE HEALTHFUL COOKING, you will need a well-stocked kitchen. You can find an extensive list of needed kitchen gadgets, as well as a lot of other useful information, on my blog *www.allergyfreetestkitchen.com* under the heading "Learning to Cook Allergy Free."

Here is a condensed version of my favorites:

- 3 to 4 liquid measuring cups
- 3 to 4 sets of dry measuring cups
- 4 to 5 sets of measuring spoons with at least one ⅛ teaspoon and ½ tablespoon
- Whisks (regular and mini), heat-resistant spatulas, and all other standard kitchen utensils
- Small and large food processor
- High-speed blender such as Ninja, Blendtec, or Vitamix
- Several glass pans of varying sizes
- 8 by 8-inch pan
- Mini loaf pans, sized 3 by 5 ½ inches
- 4 by 8-inch bread pan
- Slow cooker
- Broiler pan
- Mixing bowls
- Pots and pans
- Sharp kitchen knives
- Immersion blender
- Parchment paper (This is a must for gluten-free baked goods!)

STOCKING YOUR PANTRY

TO USE THIS COOKBOOK AND GET GREAT RESULTS, you should follow the recipes as written. I use mostly fresh and real foods that anyone can find anywhere.

The only processed foods I use (on a rare occasion) are Earth Balance Buttery Spread (dairy and soy free), Earth Balance Mindful Mayo (egg, dairy and soy free), Daiya Cheddar or Mozzarella Style Shreds, and Spectrum Organic All Vegetable Shortening (a soy-free palm oil shortening). These are now popping up on many regular supermarket shelves but can definitely be found at Whole Foods.

Most real-food advocates do not use protein powder, but I find that is one of the only ways I can have a successful grain-free and nearly sugar-free breakfast that starts my day off well.

For the gluten-free flours, I chose two commonly found (in store or online) gluten-free blends that work the best: Bob's Red Mill Gluten Free All Purpose Baking Flour (red package) and King Arthur Gluten Free All-Purpose Flour. I find cookbooks that require making your own blend to be tedious. Also, for those just dabbling in gluten-free baking, they are only required to buy one or two packages of a flour blend plus xanthan gum to make most of the recipes in this book.

There are a few recipes that require individual bags of flours, and they should not be used interchangeably, as gluten-free flours all function differently. Some of the ones I use are buckwheat, sorghum, teff, garbanzo and fava bean, and almond meal.

For sweeteners, I rely on liquid stevia, xylitol and erythritol, coconut sugar, coconut nectar, maple syrup, and honey. Xylitol and erythritol are not artificial sweeteners, but rather are naturally occurring sugar alcohols found in plants. They do not feed *Candida* and have a low glycemic index value. (Xylitol can have a laxative effect if you use too much.) You will often see me use xylitol and coconut sugar in combination. There are good reasons behind doing so—though too many to list here—so go ahead and combine! It works best that way.

When you see recipes with unsweetened coconut milk or almond milk, I am referring to the dairy-free milks that come in a carton in the refrigerated section of the supermarket (or are shelf stable). Only use canned milk if the recipe calls for it.

Coconut aminos make a good soy sauce replacement. It can be found on most large supermarket shelves, but for sure at Whole Foods. For Worcestershire sauce, I buy Lea & Perrins, as it is soy free; but it is made with shellfish, so beware if you have a shellfish allergy.

For best results, make sure to read each chapter introduction which explains the ingredients in more detail and specifies whether or not substitutions could be made.

BREAKFASTS

One of the best ways to start your day is with a breakfast of protein and healthy fats, with no or limited grains, even gluten-free ones. You will stay full longer, and it is good for weight management. That is why protein shakes are foundational to my diet. I can consume a grain-free breakfast of healthy protein and fats and stay full until lunch. It sets the tone for the whole day.

When purchasing protein powder, look for pea protein. Pea protein is one of the most easily digestible and gentle foods and has the added bonus of being grain free. Look for one that is has no sugar added or is only sweetened with stevia or xylitol. I personally like the Earth Blends varieties from Vitacost.com. NOW and Purely Inspired brands are other good choices.

That being said, a shake every day can become a bit tedious, so I do like to mix things up once in a great while with the pancakes and granola recipes found here.

The granola recipes can be adjusted to be made with regular rolled oats, if you are not concerned with consuming gluten. For gluten-free rolled oats, I like Trader Joe's or Bob's Red Mill.

CHOCOLATE PROTEIN SHAKE

Want chocolate for breakfast? No problem! This satisfying protein shake will get you through the morning until lunch.

INGREDIENTS:

1 cup unsweetened coconut milk
1 scoop chocolate pea protein powder
½ banana
5 ice cubes
1 tablespoon unsweetened cashew butter
1 tablespoon chia seeds
Handful of baby spinach (optional)

DIRECTIONS:

1. Place all ingredients in a high-speed blender and process until smooth.
2. Enjoy!

STRAWBERRY PROTEIN SHAKE

Want a berry-flavored shake? Here you go! (For an even bigger berry punch, use strawberry-flavored protein powder).

INGREDIENTS:

1 cup unsweetened coconut milk
1 scoop vanilla pea protein powder
5 large frozen strawberries
2 tablespoons flaxseed meal
1 tablespoon chia seeds
3 tablespoons water
¼ teaspoon vanilla
Handful of baby spinach (optional)

DIRECTIONS:

1. Place all ingredients in a high-speed blender and process until smooth.
2. Enjoy!

BANANA BLUEBERRY PROTEIN SHAKE

*Blueberries are so healthy and chock-full of antioxidants—
why not get a good dose at breakfast?*

INGREDIENTS:

1 cup unsweetened coconut or almond milk
1 scoop vanilla pea protein powder
½ banana
⅓ cup frozen blueberries
1 tablespoon chia seeds
3 to 5 ice cubes
Handful of baby spinach (optional)

DIRECTIONS:

1. Place all ingredients in a high-speed blender and process until smooth.
2. Enjoy!

ORANGE CREAMSICLE PROTEIN SHAKE

One of my faves—it tastes like dessert for breakfast. Add one tablespoon of orange flavored fiber powder for more orange flavor and well, fiber!

INGREDIENTS:

1 scoop vanilla pea protein powder
¾ cup unsweetened coconut milk
2 tablespoons water
¼ cup of orange juice concentrate
½ frozen banana
1 tablespoon chia seeds
Handful of baby spinach (optional)

DIRECTIONS:

1. Place all ingredients in a high-speed blender and process until smooth.
2. Enjoy!

BANANA NUTTY CHAI PROTEIN SHAKE

Need chai spice? Grab the free recipe off my blog! [http://wp.me/p2rqQv-Xe]

INGREDIENTS:

1 cup unsweetened coconut milk
1 scoop vanilla pea protein powder
⅓ teaspoon chai spice
1 tablespoon chia seeds
1 tablespoon nut butter
½ banana
3 to 5 ice cubes

DIRECTIONS:

1. Place all ingredients in a high-speed blender and process until smooth.
2. Enjoy!

BASIC GRANOLA

While called basic, this granola has anything but basic taste. It's highly addictive and free of refined sugars. You will find yourself making it over and over again.

INGREDIENTS:

¼ cup coconut oil, melted
½ cup unsweetened applesauce, warmed to room temperature
¼ cup + 1 tablespoon coconut sugar
1 teaspoon cinnamon
2 cups gluten-free rolled oats
½ cup raisins
3 tablespoons sunflower seeds

DIRECTIONS:

1. Preheat oven to 300° F.
2. In a large bowl, combine the oil, applesauce, sugar, and cinnamon.
3. Add oats and stir until all the oats are coated with wet mixture.
4. Spray a 10 by 15-inch pan with cooking spray.
5. Spread oats evenly on the pan and bake for 12 minutes.
6. Remove from oven, stir, and spread out evenly.
7. Return to oven and bake another 12 minutes.
8. Remove from oven. Sprinkle raisins and sunflower seeds over top.
9. Return to oven and bake an additional 5 minutes.
10. Let it cool before eating or storing in a sealable container.

HONEY BUNCHES GRANOLA

This irresistible granola is reminiscent of the clusters in Honey Bunches of Oats cereal. Great for breakfast, as a snack, or on top of some vegan yogurt.

INGREDIENTS:

⅓ cup honey
⅓ cup coconut oil
½ teaspoon vanilla
3 cups gluten-free rolled oats
¼ cup golden flax meal
¼ cup powdered rice milk
4 tablespoons sunflower seeds

DIRECTIONS:

1. Preheat oven to 300° F.
2. In a large glass bowl, combine honey, oil, and vanilla.
3. Microwave for 30 to 60 seconds to melt the oil and then stir to combine.
4. Add oats and stir.
5. Add flax meal and stir.
6. Add powdered rice milk and stir.
7. Spray a 10 by 15-inch pan with cooking spray.
8. Spread granola evenly on the pan.
9. Bake for 10 minutes. Then remove from the oven and stir granola.
10. Bake another 10 minutes, remove from oven, and stir. Then sprinkle on the sunflower seeds.
11. Bake for an additional 5 minutes.
12. Remove from oven. It will still feel wet, but will harden as it cools.
13. Break into bite-sized pieces.

CHOCOLATE GRANOLA

Move over, Cocoa Puffs! There is a better gluten-free chocolate "cereal" now.
This recipe was adapted from my blog to use even less sweetener,
but to be just as delicious.

INGREDIENTS:

2½ tablespoons coconut sugar
2½ tablespoons coconut oil
¼ cup unsweetened applesauce
¼ teaspoon liquid stevia
¼ cup cocoa powder
3½ cups gluten-free rolled oats
⅓ cup dairy- and soy-free chocolate chips

DIRECTIONS:

1. Preheat oven to 350° F.
2. In a large bowl, combine sugar, oil, and applesauce.
3. Microwave on high for 30 seconds or until oil is melted.
4. Add stevia and stir to combine.
5. Add cocoa powder and stir to combine.
6. Add oats and stir to coat evenly.
7. Place in oven and bake for 10 minutes.
8. Remove from oven and turn oven OFF.
9. Sprinkle chocolate chips over the top of the oats.
10. Return to oven for 2 hours, stirring every 30 minutes.
11. Cool on countertop before placing in a sealable container.
12. Store in the refrigerator.

CHOCOLATE PANCAKES WITH STRAWBERRY MAPLE SYRUP

Rich, decadent pancakes that taste like dessert without too much guilt.
After all, they are free of refined sugars.

INGREDIENTS:

½ cup sorghum flour
½ cup teff flour
⅓ cup cocoa powder
¼ cup xylitol
1½ teaspoons baking powder
¼ teaspoon salt
2 tablespoons canola oil
¼ cup unsweetened applesauce
1 cup unsweetened almond or coconut milk
2 cups whole, frozen strawberries
¼ cup pure maple syrup

DIRECTIONS:

1. In a large bowl, whisk the flours, cocoa powder, xylitol, baking powder and salt, making sure to break up any lumps of cocoa.
2. Add oil, applesauce, and milk and stir until well combined, making sure to get all dry ingredients from the bottom of the bowl.
3. Thaw the strawberries in the microwave on power 3 for 4 minutes.
4. In a small saucepan, combine the thawed berries and maple syrup.
5. Cook and stir until strawberries are finely mashed.
6. Meanwhile, use an electric griddle that has been sprayed with cooking spray to cook the pancakes.

BUCKWHEAT PANCAKES

Did you know buckwheat is a cousin to rhubarb? And if you want to get technical about it, it is not a grain, but a seed. Even better, there's no wheat or gluten in it at all, so we can call these grain-free pancakes if we really want to. So go ahead, dig in. (If you want, sorghum works in place of the garbanzo and fava bean flour, but then they won't be grain free.)

INGREDIENTS:

2 cups buttermilk (Place 2 tablespoons apple cider vinegar in a liquid measuring cup and then add unsweetened almond or coconut milk until it reaches the 2 cup line)
1½ cups buckwheat flour
½ cup garbanzo and fava bean flour
1 teaspoon baking soda
2 teaspoons baking powder
½ teaspoon salt
1 heaping teaspoon cinnamon
2 tablespoons oil
½ cup blueberry applesauce
1 tablespoon xylitol

DIRECTIONS:

1. Start by making your buttermilk.
2. Heat the griddle.
3. In a large bowl, whisk together the flours, baking soda, baking powder, salt, and cinnamon.
4. Add the oil, blueberry applesauce, and xylitol to the dry ingredients.
5. Stir in the buttermilk and continue to stir until all dry ingredients are incorporated.
6. Use a ¼-cup measuring cup to pour batter onto the hot griddle and to form pancakes.

OVERNIGHT BUCKWHEAT BREAKFAST CEREAL

This is great for summer mornings when you want something cool to eat. Just make it the evening before, let it sit in refrigerator overnight, and eat in the morning. The texture may not be for everyone (it's a bit crunchy), but it is chock-full of nutrition.

INGREDIENTS:

¼ cup Buckwheat Creamy Hot Cereal

½ cup blueberry applesauce

½ cup unsweetened coconut milk

1 tablespoon xylitol

1 tablespoon coconut sugar

¼ cup frozen blueberries

DIRECTIONS:

1. Combine all ingredients in a small bowl and place in refrigerator overnight, for at least 10 hours.
2. In the morning, it will be ready for you to enjoy!

SOUPS, CASSEROLES, ONE-DISH MEALS, AND MEATLESS MEALS

Homemade soups are the best! They make the house smell great, are full of healthy ingredients, and contain much less sodium than store-bought canned soup. Casseroles are pure comfort food and, contrary to what people think, can easily be made gluten and dairy free. And trying a meatless meal now and then is always a good practice to save money and add variety to your diet.

In any of these recipes, you can substitute the gluten-free noodles with regular wheat noodles if you are not concerned about gluten. In the recipes that call for milk or cheese alternatives like Daiya, you can substitute regular cow's milk and cheese in equal amounts; but take note, I did not test them that way. Regular mayonnaise can be substituted for Mindful Mayo.

CHICKEN NOODLE SOUP

This is not your canned soup with the red label—it is much heartier and healthier! It also works well with turkey.

INGREDIENTS:

1 tablespoon olive oil
1 cup diced celery
1 cup diced carrots
1 medium turnip, diced
1 onion, chopped
2 cups cubed, cooked chicken
4 cups chicken broth
1 teaspoon minced garlic
¼ teaspoon black pepper
½ teaspoon salt
½ teaspoon parsley flakes
1 teaspoon thyme
1½ cups gluten-free rotini pasta

DIRECTIONS:

1. In a large pot, heat oil on medium heat.
2. Add celery, carrots, turnip, and onion.
3. Sauté for 5 to 7 minutes.
4. Add cooked chicken, broth, and spices.
5. Bring to a boil and reduce heat to low and simmer with the lid on for 10 to 25 minutes.
6. Return to a boil, add pasta, and cook uncovered, on low, for 7 to 8 minutes, or until pasta is tender.

SUMMER VEGETABLE MINESTRONE SOUP

When you have a bounty of tomatoes, yellow squash, and zucchini in the late summer and early fall, this is a great soup to make. But it can also be enjoyed year round.

INGREDIENTS:

2 tablespoons oil
1 large onion, chopped
2 stalks celery, chopped
½ teaspoon minced garlic
2 cups diced fresh tomatoes
1½ teaspoons dried basil
½ teaspoon dried oregano
¼ teaspoon salt
⅛ teaspoon pepper
3 cups vegetable broth
2 cups diced yellow squash and zucchini
1 (15- to 16-ounce) can light red kidney beans, rinsed, soaked, drained, and rinsed again

DIRECTIONS:

1. Heat oil over medium-high heat.
2. Sauté onion and celery for about 5 minutes
3. Add the garlic, tomatoes, spices, and broth.
4. Bring to a boil.
5. Add zucchini, yellow squash, and the kidney beans.
6. Bring to a boil. Turn heat to low and simmer with the lid on for about 15 minutes, or until vegetables are tender.

TACO SOUP

All the flavors of taco night in a bowl!

INGREDIENTS:

1 pound ground beef
1 (15- to 16-ounce) can diced tomatoes
1 (4-ounce) can green chilis
1 tablespoon taco seasoning
1½ cups classic coleslaw mix
1½ cups beef broth
1 (15- to 16-ounce) can pinto beans, rinsed, soaked, drained and rinsed again

DIRECTIONS:

1. Brown the beef in a skillet and drain.
2. Transfer the meat to a large soup pot and add tomatoes, chilis, taco seasoning, coleslaw mix, and beef broth.
3. Bring to a boil, reduce heat, and simmer with the lid on for 20 minutes.
4. Add the pinto beans, replace the lid, and cook for an additional 10 minutes.

STOVETOP CHICKEN STEW

Do your prep ahead of time, and you can have this chicken stew on the weeknight table faster than you can imagine.

INGREDIENTS:

3 tablespoons coconut oil
3 large boneless, skinless chicken breasts, cubed
1 onion, sliced
1¼ cups diced celery
1 turnip, diced (about 1 cup)
1¼ cups sliced carrots
1 cup chicken broth
½ teaspoon dried thyme
½ teaspoon salt
1 tablespoon ketchup
1 tablespoon tapioca starch

DIRECTIONS:

1. Heat oil in a large skillet pan over medium heat.
2. Add chicken and cook and stir for about 5 minutes, until browned.
3. Add vegetables and cook and stir for about 5 minutes.
4. Meanwhile, in another bowl, combine the broth, spices, ketchup and starch.
5. Pour this mixture over the chicken and vegetables and stir.
6. Reduce heat to medium-low and put lid on skillet pan.
7. Simmer for 10 minutes, stirring occasionally, then reduce heat to low.
8. Cook until vegetables are tender and meat is done.

CHICKEN STEW
OVER MASHED POTATO BISCUITS

Reminiscent of chicken pot pie, this stew is perfect for cold, winter evenings. Full Flavor Foods and Simply Organic make gluten-free chicken gravy packets. To serve, place an opened Mashed Potato Biscuit in a bowl and top with stew. You'll thank yourself with every bite!

INGREDIENTS:

2 packets of chicken gravy mix
1½ cups sliced celery
1½ cups sliced carrots
1¼ cups frozen peas
3 cups raw, cubed, chicken
2 tablespoons tapioca starch
1 tablespoon dried, minced onion
1 teaspoon dried basil
½ teaspoon minced garlic
½ teaspoon salt
½ teaspoon pepper
2 cups water
Mashed Potato Biscuits (page 128)

DIRECTIONS:

1. Place all ingredients (except for the Mashed Potato Biscuits) in a crockpot and stir to mix.
2. Cover and cook on low for 6 to 7 hours or on high for 3½ to 4½ hours.
3. Serve over Mashed Potato Biscuits.

SPLIT PEA SOUP

I received this recipe from my friend, J, at my wedding shower many years ago. With her blessing, I am sharing it with you. It's naturally gluten and dairy free. At my house, this somehow got the name Dr. Seuss Soup.

INGREDIENTS:

2 cups dried, split green peas
6 ounces packaged diced ham
½ heaping cup diced carrots
½ cup diced celery
1 onion, chopped
1 teaspoon parsley flakes
½ teaspoon salt
¼ teaspoon pepper
¼ teaspoon thyme
1 tablespoon chicken bouillon paste or powder
5 cups water

DIRECTIONS:

1. Combine all ingredients in a large slow cooker.
2. Stir and cover.
3. Cook on low for 8 hours or on high for 4 hours.

CREAMY POTATO SOUP

You can have a thick and creamy potato soup without all the dairy (or even dairy substitutes!) and without tofu (soy). Woot! Woot! This is a favorite, time and again.

INGREDIENTS:

¼ cup olive oil
1½ cups sliced celery
1 large onion, diced
2 teaspoons minced garlic
6 cups chicken broth
½ teaspoon salt
½ tablespoon dried parsley
½ tablespoon dried chives
Dash of pepper
8 cups diced Yukon Gold potatoes
10 slices bacon, cooked and crumbled

DIRECTIONS:

1. Heat oil over medium-high heat.
2. Sauté celery and onion for about 5 minutes.
3. Add garlic, broth, and seasonings, and bring to a boil.
4. Add potatoes and boil with the lid on pan askew for 20 to 30 minutes, or until potatoes are easily pierced with a fork.
5. Remove from heat and use an immersion blender to puree most of the potatoes, leaving a few chunks.
6. Add bacon and return to stove. Keep on low heat until ready to serve.

ITALIAN CHICKEN SOUP

Grilling your chicken ahead of time takes the flavor of this soup up a notch. Either way, it's a delicious way to get your lean protein and veggies in.

INGREDIENTS:

2 tablespoons olive oil
1 cup sliced celery
1 cup diced carrots
1 medium onion, chopped
1 teaspoon minced garlic
4 cups chicken broth
1½ cups marinara sauce
½ teaspoon Italian seasoning
¼ teaspoon salt
¼ teaspoon pepper
½ cup quinoa, rinsed and drained
2 cups cubed, cooked chicken
1 (15-ounce) can black beans, rinsed, soaked, drained, and rinsed again

DIRECTIONS:

1. Heat oil in soup pot over medium heat.
2. Sauté celery, carrots, and onion for 5 to 7 minutes.
3. Add garlic, chicken broth, marinara sauce, and spices. Bring to a boil.
4. Add quinoa. Reduce heat, cover, and simmer for 15 minutes.
5. Add cooked chicken and black beans and heat for 10 minutes.

THICK AND HEARTY MINESTRONE SOUP

*Do not plan on leftovers! This soup is super satisfying
and will get eaten up in one meal.*

INGREDIENTS:

1 tablespoon oil
1 medium onion
1 teaspoon minced garlic
1 teaspoon Italian seasoning
4 cups vegetable broth
1 (14.5-ounce) can diced Italian seasoned tomatoes
1 medium zucchini
2 cups gluten-free rotini noodles
1 (15-ounce) can Great Northern beans, rinsed, soaked, drained,
    and rinsed again
2 cups chopped spinach

DIRECTIONS:

1. Heat oil in soup pot over medium heat.
2. Add onion and sauté, stirring frequently for about 4 minutes.
3. Add garlic, Italian seasoning, broth, and tomatoes. Bring to a boil.
4. Add the zucchini and cook for about 5 minutes.
5. Add the noodles and continue to boil and stir soup constantly for 4 to 6 minutes, or until noodles are tender.
6. Add the beans and boil for 2 more minutes.
7. Add the spinach and cook one minute, or until wilted.

CREAMY VEGETABLE SOUP

*While this could be called Cream of Broccoli soup, I like Creamy Vegetable Soup . . .
it makes it more enticing for kids to try. Besides, there are 5 vegetables in it.*

INGREDIENTS:

1 pound broccoli
½ pound cauliflower
1 large stalk celery
1 medium onion
1 carrot, peeled
2 cups water
2½ cups vegetable broth, divided
2 tablespoons dairy- and soy-free margarine
2 tablespoons sorghum flour
½ teaspoon salt
½ teaspoon garlic powder
⅛ teaspoon black pepper
½ cup unsweetened almond milk

DIRECTIONS:

1. Cut up broccoli and cauliflower, including the stalks.
2. Cut the celery, onion, and carrot into large chunks.
3. Bring 2 cups of water to a boil.
4. Add the vegetables and 1 cup of the broth.
5. Cook and stir until the vegetables are very soft.
6. Meanwhile, melt the margarine in a different pan over low heat.
7. Add the flour and stir to combine.
8. Add the remaining broth to the margarine and flour mixture. Set aside.
9. When the vegetables are soft, remove the pot from heat and use an immersion blender to puree all the vegetables.
10. Return the pot to the stove and add the margarine and flour mixture, spices, and almond milk. Stir to combine.
11. Heat thoroughly and serve.

BAKED ITALIAN PASTA DISH

Get all the comfort of lasagna without all the work with this easy-to-please pasta dish.

INGREDIENTS:

1 pound ground beef
1 small onion, chopped
1½ teaspoons minced garlic
1 (14.5-ounce) can stewed tomatoes
1 (6-ounce) can tomato paste
1 cup water
2 teaspoons dried parsley flakes
1 teaspoon salt
½ teaspoon black pepper
¼ teaspoon oregano
¼ teaspoon marjoram leaf
3½ cups gluten-free penne pasta
2 cups Daiya mozzarella style shreds, divided

DIRECTIONS:

1. Preheat oven to 375° F.
2. Brown the meat and onion in a skillet. Drain off the fat.
3. Add the garlic, stewed tomatoes, tomato paste, and water.
4. Add the spices and stir to mix well.
5. Simmer until thickened.
6. Meanwhile, cook the pasta until al dente.
7. In a large mixing bowl, combine cooked pasta, the meat mixture, and ¾ cup Daiya mozzarella shreds.
8. Place in a 9 by 13-inch glass pan.
9. Sprinkle remaining shreds over top of casserole.
10. Cover with foil and bake for 30 minutes.

GROUND BEEF STROGANOFF

All the flavors of stroganoff without all the dairy. Need I say more?

INGREDIENTS:

2 tablespoons olive oil
2 tablespoons potato or tapioca starch
½ cup unsweetened almond milk (or rice milk)
1 cup beef broth
1 tablespoon bottled lemon juice
1 tablespoon Dijon mustard
1½ teaspoons minced garlic
½ teaspoon salt
⅛ teaspoon pepper
½ teaspoon thyme
1 onion, chopped
1 (8-ounce) container sliced mushrooms
1 pound ground beef
3 cups dry gluten-free rotini noodles

DIRECTIONS:

1. In a pan, combine the first 10 ingredients. Cook and stir over low heat until thickened.
2. In another pan, combine the onion, mushrooms, and beef. Brown beef and drain well.
3. Use a slotted spoon to transfer the beef mixture to the sauce mixture. Stir well.
4. In a third pan, cook noodles according to package directions.
5. Serve stroganoff over noodles.

PASTA E FAGIOLI

Part soup, part pasta dish; this is pure comfort food.

INGREDIENTS:

1 tablespoon oil

1 onion, chopped

1 teaspoon minced garlic

1 teaspoon dried rosemary

2 large carrots, diced

4 cups vegetable broth

1 (14.5-ounce) can Italian flavored diced tomatoes

1½ cups gluten-free penne noodles

2 (15-ounce) cans cannellini beans, rinsed, soaked, drained, and rinsed again

DIRECTIONS:

1. In a large stockpot, heat oil over medium high heat.
2. Add onion, garlic, rosemary, and carrots.
3. Cook and stir for about 5 minutes or until vegetables are soft.
4. Add broth and tomatoes and bring to a boil.
5. Stir in pasta and cook uncovered for 7 to 8 minutes, or until al dente.
6. Add beans and heat for just a few more minutes.

TWO-POT PASTA DISH

*Remember the Hamburger Helper meals? This is reminiscent of those days;
fast, easy and delicious. Spend a little extra for the really good spaghetti sauce....
It is what makes or breaks the flavor.*

INGREDIENTS:

1 medium onion, chopped
1 pound ground beef
1 (25-ounce) jar spaghetti sauce
1 cup water
½ teaspoon minced garlic
2 cups gluten-free rotini noodles

DIRECTIONS:

1. Brown beef and onion in a skillet. Drain off the fat.
2. Pour spaghetti sauce into a large pot.
3. Pour the 1 cup water into the spaghetti sauce jar, put on the lid, and shake it around. Then add it to the sauce.
4. Bring the sauce to a boil, then add the noodles.
5. Boil with the lid on for 7 to 9 minutes, or until al dente, stirring several times to prevent noodles from sticking.
6. Add the browned meat and onion and heat thoroughly.

HOPPIN' JOHN

This southern dish makes a large amount so make it when you need quick leftovers for the next few days.

INGREDIENTS:

1 cup dry black-eyed peas
Hot tap water
8 strips bacon, cooked and crumbled
1 onion, chopped
1 (15-ounce) can no-salt-added diced tomatoes
1½ cups uncooked brown rice, rinsed and drained
1 teaspoon salt
½ teaspoon crushed red pepper
4 cups very warm tap water

DIRECTIONS:

1. Soak black-eyed peas in hot tap water for two hours, then drain, rinse, and pick over to remove any stones or debris.
2. In a large slow cooker, combine the black eyed peas with the rest of the ingredients including the 4 cups water.
3. Stir and cover.
4. Cook on low for 8 hours.

BEEF AND CABBAGE CASSEROLE

You just found a great way to sneak cabbage into your diet. I promise . . . no one will really know. If desired, you can skip the first 8 ingredients and steps 2 through 4 by using a can of condensed tomato soup in its place.

INGREDIENTS:

3 tablespoons oil
3 tablespoons starch
1 cup unsweetened almond milk (or rice milk)
½ cup tomato paste
1¼ teaspoon salt
⅛ teaspoon pepper
Dash of garlic powder
Dash of onion powder
1 pound ground beef
1 onion, chopped
1 tablespoon coconut aminos (or Worcestershire sauce)
1 cup water
¼ cup dry millet, rinsed and drained
3 cups classic coleslaw mix

DIRECTIONS:

1. Preheat oven to 350° F.
2. In a 3-quart saucepan, heat oil over medium heat and add starch.
3. Stir in milk, tomato paste, and spices.
4. Stir and cook until thick and combined.
5. In a skillet, brown the beef and onion. Drain off the fat.
6. Transfer the meat and onion to the saucepan with tomato mixture.
7. Stir in the coconut aminos, water, and millet.
8. Place the coleslaw mix on the bottom of a 2-quart casserole dish.
9. Pour tomato and meat mixture over top.
10. Cover and bake for 1 hour to 1 hour 15 minutes.

TURKEY CASSEROLE

A perfect recipe for leftover Thanksgiving Day turkey! Or make it any time of year with chicken, but turkey will remain my favorite.

INGREDIENTS:

1 tablespoon olive oil
½ cup chopped celery (about 2 stalks)
1 onion, chopped
1 small can green chilis
½ teaspoon minced garlic
1 (4-ounce) can mushrooms
2 cups cooked turkey
2 cups cooked rice (start with about ¾ cup uncooked rice)
¼ cup sorghum flour (or brown rice flour)
½ teaspoon salt
¼ teaspoon pepper
1¼ cups unsweetened original hemp milk
2 cups frozen extra fine green beans

DIRECTIONS:

1. Preheat oven to 350° F.
2. In a large skillet, heat the oil over medium high heat.
3. Sauté the celery and onion until tender, about 5 minutes.
4. Add green chilis, garlic, and mushrooms. Stir.
5. Add turkey, cooked rice, flour, salt, pepper, and hemp milk.
6. Cook and stir for 2 to 3 minutes.
7. Add the green beans and combine well.
8. Place into a 2-quart casserole dish. Cover with the lid and bake for 30 to 40 minutes, or until heated through.

TUNA CASSEROLE

This wouldn't be a cookbook without an allergy-free version of tuna casserole!

INGREDIENTS:

1 tablespoon canola oil
1 small onion, diced
¾ cup sliced mushrooms
1 celery stalk, chopped
1 cup gluten-free rotini noodles
¼ cup garbanzo bean flour (or sorghum or brown rice flour)
1¼ cups unsweetened original hemp milk
¼ cup vegetable broth
½ teaspoon salt
¼ teaspoon pepper
1 cup frozen peas
3 (5-ounce) cans tuna, packed in water, drained

DIRECTIONS:

1. Preheat oven to 400° F.
2. Heat oil in a large skillet over medium heat. Add onion, mushrooms, and celery. Sauté until soft, about 5 to 7 minutes.
3. Meanwhile, cook the pasta according to the package directions.
4. Once vegetables are done, add flour, hemp milk, broth, salt, and pepper. Cook and stir until thickened.
5. Add peas and tuna.
6. Once pasta is cooked, drain it, and add to tuna mixture. Stir well to combine.
7. Transfer to a 2-quart casserole dish.
8. Bake for 30 minutes with the cover on.

SPICY GROUND TURKEY CASSEROLE

If you are tired of all the usual ground beef recipes, give this spicy casserole using ground turkey a try!

INGREDIENTS:

1 pound ground turkey
1 onion, diced
½ cup diced baby sweet peppers (about 3)
1½ cups gluten-free penne pasta
2 cups (16 ounces) tomato sauce
1 (10-ounce) can of diced tomatoes and chilis
2 teaspoons chili powder
1½ teaspoons oregano
¼ teaspoon red pepper flakes
1 (15-ounce) can black beans, rinsed, soaked, drained, and rinsed again
1 cup Daiya Pepperjack Style Shreds, divided

DIRECTIONS:

1. Preheat oven to 350° F.
2. In a skillet, brown the turkey with the onion and peppers. Drain off all fat.
3. Meanwhile, cook the noodles.
4. Add sauce, tomatoes, and spices to the meat. Simmer for about 5 minutes.
5. Add the beans, ½ cup of the Daiya shreds, and the cooked, drained noodles. Stir to combine.
6. Place in a 2-quart casserole dish and sprinkle top of casserole with the remaining ½ cup of the Daiya shreds.
7. Bake for 20 to 25 minutes, or until bubbly.

RED BEANS AND RICE

I don't know if this qualifies as true New Orleans fare or not. But it is tasty fare if you like beans, rice, and spice! Not to mention, this is an inexpensive meal to make.

INGREDIENTS:

1 cup (about ½ pound) dry
   red beans (not kidney beans)
Water for soaking
5 cups water, divided
1 cup uncooked brown rice
1 cup vegetable broth
4 tablespoons grapeseed oil, divided
1 onion, diced
1 celery stalk, sliced

1 green pepper, chopped
1½ teaspoons thyme
1½ teaspoons onion powder
1½ teaspoons hot sauce
½ teaspoon liquid smoke
½ teaspoon black pepper
¼ teaspoon cayenne pepper
1 tablespoon coconut sugar

DIRECTIONS:

1. Place beans in a dish and cover with water and a lid. Place in the refrigerator overnight.
2. The next day, drain the beans and rinse well. Pick out any stones or debris.
3. Place beans in a skillet with 4 cups of the water. Bring to a boil. Reduce heat to medium-low and cook with the lid slightly askew. Stir occasionally and add water as needed. Cook for about an hour, or until beans are easily pierced with a fork.
4. Meanwhile, start cooking the brown rice in the remaining 1 cup of water and 1 cup broth. Follow package directions for the cooking time. Set aside when done.
5. When the beans are soft, drain and rinse with hot tap water in a colander.
6. Wipe out the skillet with paper towel.
7. Heat 3 tablespoons oil in the skillet and cook and stir the onion, celery, and pepper until soft and just starting to brown.
8. Add the spices, beans, and remaining 1 tablespoon oil. Stir to coat.
9. Warm on low heat until heated through and the rice is ready.
10. When ready to eat, top rice with the beans.

SPINACH AND BEAN BURRITOS

Head to my blog, Allergy-Free Test Kitchen, and grab the free recipe entitled Gluten-Free Tortillas and double it for this burrito recipe. [http://wp.me/p2rqQv-Ja] (Or purchase gluten-free wraps). Then enjoy this comforting, meatless meal.

INGREDIENTS:

4 large tortilla wraps
1 (15- to 16-ounce) can light red kidney beans, rinsed, soaked, drained, and rinsed again
1½ cups mild salsa
½ cup refried beans
1 (10-ounce) box frozen spinach, thawed and drained
Unsweetened coconut milk yogurt (optional)
Daiya Pepperjack Style Shreds

DIRECTIONS:

1. Prepare your tortillas if making your own.
2. Preheat oven to 375° F and spray a 9 by 13-inch glass pan with cooking spray.
3. In a bowl, combine the kidney beans, salsa, and refried beans.
4. Lay a wrap on a plate.
5. Spoon some yogurt down the middle of the wrap, if using.
6. Put one-quarter of the spinach on the wrap.
7. Place about one-quarter of the bean mixture on top of the spinach.
8. Sprinkle with a little of the Daiya shreds.
9. Roll up and place seam side down in prepared pan.
10. Repeat steps 4 through 9 three more times, making sure to reserve some of the bean mixture.
11. Pour the remaining bean mixture over top of burritos. Sprinkle with Daiya shreds.
12. Bake for 10 minutes.

BLACK BEAN, VEGETABLE, AND RICE CASSEROLE

Don't let beans scare you away from this casserole which feels like comfort food in a flash.

INGREDIENTS:

½ cup dry brown rice
2 cups mild salsa
1 zucchini, chopped
1 cup chopped broccoli
1 red pepper, diced
1 (15-ounce) can black beans, rinsed, soaked, drained, and rinsed again
Daiya mozzarella shreds (optional)

DIRECTIONS:

1. Cook the rice according to package directions.
2. Preheat oven to 350° F.
3. In a skillet, heat salsa over medium heat.
4. Add the vegetables and cook for about 10 minutes.
5. Add in beans and cooked rice. Simmer on low for 5 minutes.
6. Place the mixture in a 2-quart casserole dish.
7. Top with Daiya shreds, if using.
8. Bake, uncovered, for about 20 minutes, or until bubbly.

RICE AND BEAN WRAPS

I love using this easy meatless meal in the summer when I don't feel like doing a lot of cooking. Get a free recipe for gluten-free tortillas on my blog, Allergy-Free Test Kitchen. [http://wp.me/p2rqQv-Ja]

INGREDIENTS:

1 cup cooked brown rice (about 1/3 cup dry rice)
1 (15- to 16-ounce) can light red kidney beans, rinsed, soaked, drained, and
    rinsed again
1 cup refried beans
1 Roma tomato, chopped
½ teaspoon minced garlic
1 yellow baby sweet pepper
1 tablespoon dried minced onion
½ cup salsa
Gluten-free tortilla wraps

DIRECTIONS:

1. Mix all the ingredients (except the tortillas) in a skillet.
2. Heat over medium-low until heated through.
3. Serve in a warm tortilla wrap.

SPAGHETTI AND CHICKPEA BALLS

These little meatless "meatballs" are fun to make and taste great with a high-quality marinara sauce.

INGREDIENTS:

1 (15-ounce) can chickpeas, rinsed, soaked, drained, and rinsed again
¼ cup garbanzo and fava bean flour (or sorghum or brown rice flour)
1 tablespoon dried parsley
1 tablespoon dried minced onion
1 tablespoon minced garlic
½ tablespoon bottled lemon juice
½ tablespoon olive oil
1½ teaspoons oregano
1 teaspoon marjoram
¼ teaspoon pepper
Spaghetti noodles
Spaghetti sauce

DIRECTIONS:

1. Place all the ingredients (except the noodles and sauce) in a food processor.
2. Process until well mixed.
3. Remove the blade and put the mixture in the refrigerator for about an hour.
4. Preheat oven to 400° F.
5. Line a cookie sheet with aluminum foil and spray with cooking spray.
6. Form the chickpea mixture into 18 balls.
7. Place them onto the cookie sheet and bake for 10 minutes.
8. Remove from the oven and turn each ball over. Bake an additional 10 minutes.
9. Meanwhile, cook your spaghetti and heat your sauce.
10. Serve chickpea balls with noodles and sauce.

ENTREES

Whether you like beef, pork, or chicken, I've got you covered in this chapter. I like the slow cooker a lot because it makes for easy prep and cooking. But there is a trick to slow cooker cooking. . . . Don't peek! Seriously, do not lift the lid—ever! Once that lid is on, keep it on. Removing the lid removes moisture and so much heat that it ends up drying out the food and extending the cooking time. So I say it again, no peeking!

In any recipe that calls for gluten-free oats, you can substitute regular oats if you are not concerned about gluten. If you consume soy, you can use soy sauce in place of the coconut aminos; but beware, I did not test the recipes that way. Lea & Perrins Original Worcestershire Sauce is soy free, but does contain shellfish.

HAMBURGER PATTIES

Sometimes it is best to NOT replace your gluten-filled bun with a gluten-free one. Eating a hamburger with a fork and knife allows for other flavors to shine through. Plus, you will eat fewer calories; your hips will thank you.

INGREDIENTS:

1 pound ground beef
⅓ cup gluten-free rolled oats
2 tablespoons dried onion soup mix
2 teaspoons Worcestershire sauce

DIRECTIONS:

1. Mix all ingredients well.
2. Form into 4 patties.
3. Grill over medium heat, flipping once, until internal temperature reaches 160° to 170° F.

SLOPPY JOE PIZZA

*Sloppy Joes plus pizza...what more could you ask for? Make your own gluten-free pizza crust (Cybele Pascal has an awesome one in **The Allergen-Free Baker's Handbook**) or buy pre-made pizza crusts for a quicker meal. This makes enough to cover two (9-inch) pizza crusts. Alternatively, this Sloppy Joe mixture could be served on hamburger buns as well.*

INGREDIENTS:

1 pound ground beef
1 (6-ounce) can tomato paste
1 cup beef broth
2 tablespoons dried minced onion
2 tablespoons tapioca starch
½ teaspoon chili powder
¼ teaspoon pepper
¼ teaspoon garlic powder
2 (9-inch) gluten-free pizza crusts
Daiya mozzarella or cheddar style shreds (optional)

DIRECTIONS:

1. Heat oven to the temperature needed for the selected type of pizza crust.
2. Brown meat and drain off all fat.
3. Add all the ingredients (except pizza crusts) to the meat.
4. Cook over low heat, stirring occasionally, until combined and warm.
5. Transfer meat mixture to pizza crusts and spread out evenly.
6. Sprinkle with Daiya, if using.
7. Bake according to the instructions for the selected type of pizza crust.

VEGGIE-PACKED MEATLOAF

Better than traditional meatloaf. Seriously, you'll be pleasantly surprised.
The secret lies, not only in the ingredients, but in the method—so follow directions.
Don't go rogue on me.

INGREDIENTS:

1 pound ground beef
1 teaspoon salt
⅛ teaspoon pepper
¼ cup chopped onion,
½ cup finely chopped broccoli
¾ cups gluten-free rolled oats
1 (5.5-ounce) can of low-sodium vegetable juice

DIRECTIONS:

1. Preheat oven to 350° F.
2. Line the bottom of a broiler pan with aluminum foil.
3. Place the rack on top and use cooking spray to spray the half where the meatloaf will be placed.
4. In a large bowl, combine all ingredients, using your hands to mix thoroughly.
5. Shape the mixture into a loaf shape on the broiler rack where cooking spray was applied.
6. Bake for 1 hour.

BEEF BURGUNDY OVER MASHED POTATOES

*No need to buy expensive wine to cook this dish: the cooking wine available in the salad dressing aisle works just fine. And don't worry—
this is safe for the under-21 crowd.*

INGREDIENTS:

1½ pounds beef stew meat
1 large onion, sliced
1 (8-ounce) container of sliced mushrooms
½ cup ketchup
⅓ cup water
⅓ cup Burgundy cooking wine
2 tablespoons coconut aminos
2 tablespoons coconut sugar
1½ teaspoons paprika
1 teaspoon salt
½ teaspoon dried mustard powder
½ teaspoon minced garlic
Mashed potatoes (page 75)

DIRECTIONS:

1. Cut visible fat from beef stew meat.
2. Place in slow cooker.
3. Top with onion and mushrooms.
4. In a bowl, combine the rest of the ingredients (except mashed potatoes).
5. Pour over meat and vegetables.
6. Cook on low for 8 hours or on high for 4 hours.
7. To serve, place meat and vegetables over mashed potatoes.

GRILLED SHOULDER STEAK

*When shoulder steaks go on the $5 meat sale, I grab a bunch and freeze them.
Then whenever the desire for a grilled meal strikes, these satisfy that craving.
Whatever you do . . . don't skip the marinating time.*

INGREDIENTS:

1 to 2 shoulder steaks, thawed if frozen
½ cup olive oil
1 tablespoon Chicago Steak Seasoning
2 tablespoons coconut aminos
2 teaspoons minced garlic

DIRECTIONS:

1. Place meat in a glass pan with a lid.
2. In a separate bowl, mix the rest of the ingredients and pour over meat.
3. Marinate, covered, for at least 6 hours, turning meat at least once.
4. Grill over medium heat until cooked to desired doneness.

EASY BEEF TIPS

Dump in the ingredients, turn on the slow cooker, and relax.
Five hours later, you'll be enjoying this tasty meal.

INGREDIENTS:

1 pound beef stew meat
1¼ cups baby pearl onions
½ red pepper, diced
1½ cups tomato basil spaghetti sauce
½ teaspoon minced garlic
¼ cup beef broth
Hot, cooked rice or gluten-free rotini noodles

DIRECTIONS:

1. Trim any visible fat from meat and cut into bite-sized pieces, if necessary.
2. Place meat in a slow cooker.
3. Place onions and pepper over the meat.
4. Mix spaghetti sauce, garlic, and beef broth. Pour over the meat.
5. Cook in the slow cooker for 5 hours on high temperature.
6. Serve with rice or noodles.

MEXICAN MEATBALLS

*This is one of the first recipes I have ever created for a recipe contest.
Even though I didn't win, the recipe is a winner for taking meatballs to a spicy level.*

INGREDIENTS:

1 pound ground beef
1 tablespoon dried minced onion
1 (4.5-ounce) can mild green chilis
1 teaspoon chili powder
1 teaspoon oregano
1 teaspoon cumin
¼ teaspoon garlic powder
2 cups mild salsa

DIRECTIONS:

1. Preheat oven to 350° F.
2. Place meat in a bowl.
3. Add chilis and spices and mix thoroughly using your hands.
4. Shape into 11 to 12 balls and place in a 2-quart casserole dish.
5. Pour salsa over meatballs.
6. Cover with a lid and bake for one hour.

OVEN-ROASTED FLANK STEAK

I like to make this on Sunday afternoons in winter since the oven needs to be on for 3 hours. I purchase flank steaks when they are reduced for quick sale at the grocery store; otherwise they can be quite pricey.

INGREDIENTS:

1 (1½-pound) flank steak
1 (28-ounce) can whole, peeled tomatoes
1 onion, wedged in 8 pieces
½ cup beef broth
¼ cup cooking Burgundy cooking wine
½ teaspoon oregano
½ teaspoon parsley
½ teaspoon marjoram
¼ teaspoon salt
¼ teaspoon pepper

DIRECTIONS:

1. Preheat oven to 350° F.
2. Trim fat from the meat.
3. Place meat and onions in a small roasting pan with a lid.
4. Place the tomatoes in a bowl and snip into smaller pieces with a food scissors.
5. Add broth, wine, and spices to the tomatoes. Stir to combine.
6. Pour the mixture over meat and cover with a lid.
7. Roast for 3 hours.

SLOW COOKER ROAST

So easy to put together and so delicious to eat—the hardest part is waiting 8 hours!

INGREDIENTS:

 1 (2-pound) bottom round roast (size can vary)
 1 package dried onion soup mix
 1 cup water
 ¼ cup coconut aminos

DIRECTIONS:

1. Cut as much visible fat from the meat as possible.
2. Place meat in a slow cooker.
3. Sprinkle with the dried onion soup mix.
4. Add water and coconut aminos.
5. Cook on low for 8 hours.

MEATBALLS WITH BEEF GRAVY

So simple, yet so comforting, this recipe comes together very fast and is perfect for a weeknight meal.

INGREDIENTS:

1 pound ground beef
½ cup gluten-free rolled oats
¼ cup unsweetened almond milk (or rice milk)
½ teaspoon salt
½ teaspoon coconut aminos or Worcestershire sauce
¼ teaspoon pepper
1 tablespoon dried minced onion

GRAVY:

2 tablespoons dairy- and soy-free margarine
1 tablespoon dried minced onion
2 tablespoons sorghum flour (or brown rice flour)
1 cup beef broth

DIRECTIONS:

1. Preheat oven to 400° F.
2. Line the bottom of a broiler pan with aluminum foil. Spray the broiler rack with cooking spray.
3. In a bowl, combine the meatball ingredients. Shape into about 14 balls.
4. Place the meatballs on the broiler pan and bake for 20 to 22 minutes.
5. Meanwhile, to make gravy, melt margarine in a small saucepan over medium-low heat.
6. Add onion and flour. Stir to combine.
7. Add beef broth. Bring to a boil and stir constantly until thick.
8. Serve meatballs with gravy.

SWEET AND SOUR BEEF WITH CARROTS

Haul out your slow cooker for another "easy to put together" (and delicious) meal.

INGREDIENTS:

2 pounds beef stew meat
1 onion, sliced
1 package baby carrots
⅓ cup ketchup
⅓ cup xylitol
½ teaspoon liquid stevia
¼ cup red wine vinegar
1 tablespoon coconut aminos
1 cup beef broth

DIRECTIONS:

1. Trim fat from meat and cut into bite-sized pieces.
2. Place in slow cooker. Place onion and carrots on top of meat.
3. In a large liquid measuring cup, combine the ketchup, xylitol, stevia, vinegar, coconut aminos, and broth.
4. Pour the ketchup mixture over the meat and vegetables.
5. Cook on low for 8 hours.

PORK PATTIES WITH AWESOME SAUCE

Get ready to have your socks knocked off! These patties taste like grilled meatloaf. Topped with the sauce, you will never miss a bun (gluten free or not).

INGREDIENTS:

1 pound ground pork
½ cup gluten-free rolled oats
1 (4-ounce) can green chilis
1 tablespoon dried minced onion
1 tablespoon Dijon mustard
1 tablespoon coconut aminos
⅓ teaspoon salt
⅛ teaspoon garlic powder

SAUCE:

⅓ cup ketchup
1 tablespoon Dijon mustard
1 tablespoon coconut sugar
½ tablespoon xylitol
¼ teaspoon apple cider vinegar

DIRECTIONS:

1. Heat grill.
2. In a large bowl, combine the ingredients for the patties.
3. Mix well and form into 4 to 5 large patties.
4. In a small saucepan, combine the sauce ingredients.
5. Heat the sauce over low heat for about 10 to 15 minutes, stirring occasionally.
6. Grill the patties over medium heat for 7 minutes. Flip and cook for an additional 8 minutes or until patties reach an internal temperature of 160° F.
7. Serve the patties topped with the sauce.

SLOW COOKER BONELESS RIBS

Get the taste of ribs without all the messy bones in this simple yet delicious slow cooker meal. (Is it hard to tell I like simple? And slow cookers?)

INGREDIENTS:

3 pounds boneless pork spareribs
½ cup ketchup
⅓cup coconut sugar
¼ cup water
1 tablespoon apple cider vinegar
1 tablespoon coconut aminos (or Worcestershire sauce)

DIRECTIONS:

1. Trim all visible fat from meat.
2. Place ribs in a slow cooker.
3. In a liquid measuring cup, combine the ketchup, sugar, water, vinegar, and coconut aminos.
4. Pour the sauce mixture over ribs.
5. Cover and cook on low for 6 hours.

GLAZED HAM STEAK

This is super-fast and easy for a weeknight meal. For a holiday meal, simply increase the ingredients of the glaze to your liking to accommodate a large ham. I've been told this is the best ham glaze ever.

INGREDIENTS:

¼ cup apricot jam
2½ tablespoons coconut sugar
¾ teaspoon dried ground mustard
1 (1-pound) ham steak

DIRECTIONS:

1. Combine the jam, sugar, and mustard in a small saucepan.
2. Cook over low heat until well combined and smooth.
3. Prepare the ham according to the package directions.
4. Spread glaze over ham steak and serve.

PORK CHOPS AND POTATO DINNER

Creamy comfort food (that's dairy free!) at its best. What more could you ask for?

INGREDIENTS:

1 cup finely chopped mushrooms
3 tablespoons + 2 teaspoons olive oil, divided
3 tablespoons tapioca starch (or any starch)
1 cup unsweetened almond milk (or rice milk)
1 cup chicken broth
3 tablespoons Dijon mustard
¾ teaspoon salt
1¾ teaspoons dried basil
¼ teaspoon thyme
⅛ teaspoon pepper
1 pound (about 5) red potatoes, diced into bite-sized pieces
4 boneless pork chops
½ onion, sliced

DIRECTIONS:

1. Sauté mushrooms in 2 teaspoons of the oil.
2. In a separate saucepan, heat the remaining 3 tablespoons of the oil over medium heat.
3. Add starch and stir to combine.
4. Add milk and cook and stir until bubbly.
5. Add sautéed mushrooms and stir to combine.
6. Add broth, mustard, and spices to the mushroom mixture. Cook and stir until well combined.
7. Place the cut-up potatoes into a large crockpot.
8. Trim fat off of boneless pork chops and nestle the meat into the potatoes.
9. Place the onion on top.
10. Pour mushroom and broth mixture over contents of crockpot.
11. Cook on low for 8 hours.

STOVETOP TUSCAN CHICKEN

Fancy enough for Sunday dinner and easy enough for a weeknight meal, this is a fast and delicious way to prepare chicken.

INGREDIENTS:

2 tablespoons coconut oil

12 to 13 boneless, skinless chicken tenders

1 onion, sliced

1 (15- to 16-ounce) can diced tomatoes

¼ cup white cooking wine

1 teaspoon minced garlic

1½ teaspoons Italian Seasoning Blend

½ teaspoon salt

¼ teaspoon crushed red pepper flakes

DIRECTIONS:

1. Heat oil in a skillet pan over medium heat.
2. Add chicken tenders and onion slices. Cook, turning frequently, until the chicken is browned on all sides.
3. Add tomatoes, cooking wine, garlic, and spices.
4. Cover, turn heat to low, and cook for 10 to 15 minutes, flipping chicken pieces over occasionally.

CRUNCHY CHICKEN TENDERS

Who needs drive-through chicken tenders when you can make your own healthier, gluten-free version fast and easy? Kids will love these, as will parents.

INGREDIENTS:

1 pound chicken tenders
2½ cups gluten-free rice Chex cereal
¼ cup dairy- and soy-free margarine (or more, as needed)
½ teaspoon onion powder

DIRECTIONS:

1. Preheat oven to 400° F.
2. Trim any fat from the chicken tenders.
3. In a flat, shallow dish, crush the cereal with the bottom side of a glass.
4. In another flat dish, melt the margarine in microwave.
5. Add onion powder to the melted margarine.
6. Dip a chicken tender in the margarine. Then coat with crumbs and place on a cookie sheet. Repeat with the other tenders, using additional margarine if necessary.
7. Bake for 20 to 30 minutes, or until done.

GARLIC AND COCONUT-SUGAR CHICKEN

I love slow cooker meals because they are so easy to prepare and there is no rushing around right before meal time. This dish, while different, will not disappoint.

INGREDIENTS:

3 pounds boneless chicken thighs
½ cup coconut sugar
½ cup white cooking wine
1 tablespoon bottled lemon juice
½ tablespoon bottled lime juice
1 tablespoon minced garlic
1 tablespoon coconut aminos
½ teaspoon black pepper

DIRECTIONS:

1. Trim fat off of chicken thighs and place in a slow cooker.
2. In a bowl, combine the sugar, wine, lemon and lime juices, garlic, coconut aminos, and pepper. Pour over chicken.
3. Cook on low for 6 hours.

SLOW COOKER HAWAIIAN CHICKEN

Who doesn't love a slow-cooked meal after a long day?
Enjoy this meal any time of year for a taste of Hawaii.

INGREDIENTS:

4 boneless chicken breasts
4 canned pineapple rings
12 canned mandarin orange slices
¼ cup pineapple juice (from the can)
½ cup mandarin orange juice (from the can)
⅓ cup coconut sugar
2 tablespoons bottled lemon juice
¼ cup tapioca starch (or any starch)
½ teaspoon minced garlic
¼ teaspoon powdered ginger
Hot, cooked brown rice

DIRECTIONS:

1. Spray the crockpot with cooking spray.
2. Place chicken breasts in the crockpot.
3. Cover each breast with a pineapple ring and mandarin oranges
4. In a small bowl, combine the rest of the ingredients (except rice).
5. Pour over the chicken and fruit.
6. Cook on low for 4 to 5 hours.
7. Serve over hot, cooked brown rice.

GRILLED CHICKEN WITH PLUM SAUCE

*Here's a fun twist on grilled chicken. I make it when plums
are in season and on the cheap at $0.19 a plum!*

INGREDIENTS:

1 teaspoon coconut oil

1½ teaspoons minced garlic

¾ teaspoon powdered ginger

3 plums, pitted and chopped

2 tablespoons coconut sugar

2 tablespoons water

1 tablespoon coconut aminos, or Worcestershire sauce

4 boneless chicken breasts

DIRECTIONS:

1. Combine all the ingredients (except chicken) in a small saucepan.
2. Turn heat to medium-low and bring to a boil, stirring occasionally.
3. Once the mixture boils, turn heat to low. Continue to stir and cook for 35 to 40 minutes, or until all plum chunks are soft and broken up.
4. Grill the chicken breasts. (Or bake them on a cookie sheet in a 400° F oven for 30 minutes, if grilling isn't an option.)
5. To serve, slice the chicken breasts and pour plum sauce on top.

CRANBERRY SALSA CHICKEN

This stovetop skillet dish comes together fast. It tastes wonderful with rice or quinoa and broccoli or green beans.

INGREDIENTS:

1¼ cups mild salsa

⅔ cup dried cranberries

¼ cup water

9 drops liquid stevia

1 teaspoon minced garlic

½ teaspoon cinnamon

¼ teaspoon cumin

1 tablespoon coconut oil

4 boneless, thin-cut chicken breasts

Hot, cooked brown rice

DIRECTIONS:

1. In a small bowl, combine all the ingredients (except oil, chicken and rice). Stir and set aside.
2. Heat the oil over medium-high heat in a skillet pan with a lid.
3. Place the chicken breasts in a pan and brown both sides of each chicken breast.
4. Reduce heat to medium-low and pour the salsa and cranberry mixture over the top.
5. Place a lid on the skillet and cook the chicken for a total of 10 to 15 minutes, turning over breasts and scooping salsa mixture over them every 4 to 5 minutes.
6. Serve with hot, cooked brown rice.

OVEN-ROASTED CHICKEN THIGHS

Simple enough for a weeknight meal and elegant enough for company, you will love this easy-to-prepare chicken dish. It will soon become a favorite.

INGREDIENTS:

6 chicken thighs, skin removed
2 tablespoons olive oil
½ teaspoon oregano
½ teaspoon thyme
¼ teaspoon salt
¼ teaspoon pepper

DIRECTIONS:

1. Preheat oven to 375° F.
2. Place chicken thighs in a 9 by 13-inch glass pan.
3. Pour oil over the chicken.
4. Using tongs, turn the thighs over to coat all sides of the chicken. Turn so the meaty side is up.
5. Sprinkle the spices evenly over the thighs.
6. Roast in oven for 30 to 45 minutes, or until the internal temperature is 180° F.

ALMOST-GRILLED SALMON FILETS

I love the salmon at Aldi stores because they run about $3.89 per 16-ounce bag, are wild caught, and certified sustainable seafood by MSC.org. Preparing these salmon filets on the broiler pan gives them a grilled-like taste.

INGREDIENTS:

1 (16-ounce) package salmon filets
2 tablespoons dairy- and soy-free margarine
Lemon pepper seasoning

DIRECTIONS:

1. Set the top oven rack so it is about 4 to 5 inches from the top heating element.
2. Set the oven to broil.
3. Melt the margarine in the microwave.
4. Lay a piece of aluminum foil on the bottom of a broiler pan.
5. Lay the broiler pan rack on top and spray with cooking spray.
6. Place the salmon filets on the broiler pan and brush evenly with about half of the melted margarine.
7. Sprinkle the tops of the filets with lemon pepper seasoning, using as much or as little as you like.
8. Broil with the oven door open for 5 minutes.
9. Remove pan from oven and gently flip each filet over.
10. Brush with the remaining melted margarine and sprinkle lemon pepper seasoning over the top.
11. Broil 6 more minutes.
12. When the fish flakes easily with a fork, it is done.

SALADS, SIDES, AND VEGETABLES

Eat more vegetables! Seriously, most people do not eat enough. And when you buy the frozen varieties with added sauces and flavors, you are taking away the vegetables' nutritional value by adding so much salt, dairy, and artificial ingredients. Making your own vegetables that taste great is not difficult, so I've included a lot of basic recipes. Just follow the easy instructions, and you will start to love your vegetables.

In the recipes that include Mindful Mayo, you can substitute regular mayonnaise in equal parts.

BAKED FRUIT SALAD

Perfect for winter days and even holidays, this baked fruit salad tastes great eaten warm. Any leftovers you may have taste great cold, too. It also freezes well.

INGREDIENTS:

1 (14- to 15-ounce) can red tart cherries in water

1 tablespoon tapioca starch (or any starch)

2 tablespoons coconut sugar

1½ teaspoons vanilla

¼ teaspoon salt

18 drops liquid stevia

1 (20-ounce) can pineapple chunks, drained

1 (15-ounce) can pears, drained and cut into slices, if necessary

1 (15-ounce) can peaches, drained and cut into slices, if necessary

1 (11-ounce) can mandarin oranges, drained

1 cup unsweetened applesauce

3 tablespoons coconut sugar

2 teaspoons cinnamon

DIRECTIONS:

1. In a saucepan, combine the first 6 ingredients listed. Cook over medium heat, stirring often, until thickened. Set aside.
2. Preheat oven to 325° F.
3. In a large bowl, combine the cherry mixture with the remaining ingredients.
4. Pour into a 9 by 13-inch glass pan.
5. Bake for about 60 minutes.
6. Serve warm, but it can also be enjoyed cold.

SWEET PEA SALAD

Bacon? Why, yes! Salty bacon with sweet raisins will get anyone to eat their peas in this salad that will disappear faster than you can say, "Eat your peas."

INGREDIENTS:

2 cups frozen peas, thawed
7 strips of bacon, cooked and crumbled
½ cup golden raisins
1 tablespoon dried minced onion
⅔ cup Earth Balance Mindful Mayo
1 tablespoon apple cider vinegar
½ heaping teaspoon xylitol

DIRECTIONS:

1. Toss peas, bacon, raisins, and dried onion in a bowl.
2. In a small food processor, combine Mindful Mayo, vinegar, and xylitol.
3. Coat the salad with the dressing and cover with plastic wrap.
4. Refrigerate at least two hours before serving.

COLESLAW

Cabbage is an underutilized vegetable, and it's so good for people! So if I have to add some Mindful Mayo to make it go down the hatch, I will. It's better than not being eaten at all! I make this when I have coleslaw mix on hand from making Taco Soup or Beef and Cabbage Casserole.

INGREDIENTS:

4 cups coleslaw mix
½ cup Mindful Mayo
1 tablespoon erythritol (or xylitol)
1 tablespoon dried minced onion
2 teaspoons bottled lemon juice
2 teaspoons Dijon mustard
⅛ teaspoon salt
⅛ teaspoon pepper

DIRECTIONS:

1. Place coleslaw mix in a bowl.
2. In a small food processor, combine the remaining ingredients.
3. Pour over the coleslaw mix and stir to coat completely.
4. Refrigerate for at least 2 hours before serving.

CANDY APPLE WALDORF SALAD

Waldorf salad is rumored to be named after a salad created in 1893 by the Waldorf Astoria Hotel of New York City. I took the Waldorf salad of my youth and switched it up to be allergy friendly and free of refined sugars. The taste is like candied apples. . . . It's quite decadent.

INGREDIENTS:

1 small head of green lettuce
1 apple, chopped
½ cup raisins
⅓cup sunflower seeds
½ cup Earth Balance Mindful Mayo
⅓ cup coconut sugar

DIRECTIONS:

1. Wash lettuce, let it dry, and tear it into bite sized pieces.
2. In a large bowl, toss the lettuce with the apple, raisins, and sunflower seeds.
3. In a separate bowl, mix the Mindful Mayo with sugar. Pour it onto the salad and stir to coat completely.
4. Serve immediately.

POTATO SALAD

Someone once told me they thought they had to purchase pre-made potato salad, as though it were a hard and fast rule. I say, "Nonsense—make your own!" It's not that difficult, and you will win over any crowd. Guaranteed.

INGREDIENTS:

2 pounds red potatoes
⅓ cup diced red onion
⅓ cup chopped celery
⅓ cup pickle relish
1 tablespoon dried parsley
⅔ cup Earth Balance Mindful Mayo
1 tablespoon bottled lemon juice
1 tablespoon Dijon mustard
½ teaspoon salt
¼ teaspoon pepper
⅛ teaspoon garlic powder
⅛ teaspoon onion powder

DIRECTIONS:

1. Scrub the potatoes, but do not peel.
2. Cut the potatoes into bite-sized pieces.
3. Place the potatoes in a pot and cover with water.
4. Bring to a boil and boil with the lid askew for 7 to 10 minutes, or until the potatoes are tender.
5. Drain and then cool the potatoes on a cookie sheet.
6. In a large bowl, place the onion, celery, relish, and parsley. Add the potatoes.
7. In a small bowl, combine the Mindful Mayo with the lemon juice, mustard, and spices.
8. Pour the mayo mixture over the potatoes and stir to cover completely.
9. Refrigerate for several hours before serving.

MASHED POTATOES

Who says you need milk and butter to make fabulous mashed potatoes?
Not me! Hemp milk makes these thicker and creamier, but
unsweetened almond milk works, too.

INGREDIENTS:

3 large russet potatoes
2 tablespoons dairy- and soy-free margarine
½ teaspoon salt
¼ teaspoon pepper
¾ cup unsweetened, original hemp milk

DIRECTIONS:

1. Scrub and peel potatoes.
2. Cut into small pieces.
3. Place in a large pan and cover with water.
4. Put a lid on the pan and bring to a boil.
5. Boil with the lid askew, 10 to 12 minutes, or until the potato pieces are really soft.
6. Drain in a colander.
7. In a stand mixer, beat the potatoes with margarine, salt, and pepper, until crumbly.
8. Add milk and beat until smooth and creamy.

SAVORY SWEET POTATO FRIES WITH DIPPING SAUCE

Sweet potatoes are often prepared, well, sweet. Twist it up with this savory version of sweet potato fries with a dip. You'll thank me.

INGREDIENTS:

2 sweet potatoes
1½ tablespoons olive oil
1 teaspoon chili powder
⅓ teaspoon cumin

DIP:

¼ cup + 2 tablespoons Earth Balance Mindful Mayo
½ tablespoon unsweetened almond milk
⅜ teaspoon dried minced onion
¼ teaspoon garlic powder

DIRECTIONS:

1. Preheat oven to 425° F.
2. Scrub and peel the sweet potatoes and cut into steak fries.
3. In a bowl, combine the oil, chili powder, and cumin.
4. Place the fries in the bowl and toss to combine.
5. Place on a baking stone, spread them out, and bake for 20 minutes, or until easily pierced with a fork.
6. Meanwhile, in a small bowl, combine the dipping sauce ingredients.
7. Serve the fries with the dipping sauce.

ROASTED ASPARAGUS

My favorite way to cook asparagus is grilling the thick stalks directly on the grates, but this is a close second when only the thin stalks are available.

INGREDIENTS:

1 pound asparagus
2 tablespoons melted coconut oil
1 teaspoon bottled lemon juice
¼ teaspoon garlic powder

DIRECTIONS:

1. Preheat oven to 400° F.
2. Wash asparagus and cut off the bottom ½ inch of each stalk.
3. Place asparagus in a 9 by 13-inch glass pan.
4. Evenly pour the melted oil over the asparagus.
5. Sprinkle the asparagus evenly with lemon juice and then the garlic powder.
6. Roast in the oven, uncovered, for 30 to 40 minutes, or until tender.

SLOW COOKER GREEN BEANS, POTATOES, AND BACON

Bacon makes everything great! And this recipe is no exception. Here is a great vegetable dish to make for company because you can prepare it ahead of time and not be fussing in the kitchen when you could be visiting.

INGREDIENTS:

1 pound fresh green beans, ends snapped off

3 medium red potatoes, chopped into bite-sized pieces

1 onion, chopped

6 slices of bacon, cooked

1 teaspoon xylitol

1 teaspoon salt

1½ cup vegetable broth (or chicken broth)

DIRECTIONS:

1. In the bottom of the slow cooker, place the beans.
2. On top of the beans, place the potatoes.
3. Then place the onion on top of potatoes and the cooked bacon on very top.
4. In a small bowl, mix the xylitol, salt, and broth together.
5. Pour the broth mixture over the vegetables.
6. Cook on low for 4 hours.

OVEN-ROASTED ZUCCHINI SQUASH

*There's something about roasting that brings out the sweetness in vegetables.
This will get gobbled up faster than you can wink.*

INGREDIENTS:

1 yellow summer squash
1 zucchini
2 tablespoons grapeseed oil
Salt and pepper to season
½ cup Daiya mozzarella shreds (optional)

DIRECTIONS:

1. Preheat oven to 400° F.
2. Cut squash and zucchini into ¼-inch-thick rounds.
3. Spread on a 10 by 15-inch pan.
4. Toss with oil and season with salt and pepper.
5. Roast in the oven for 18 minutes.
6. Sprinkle Daiya shreds over the top, if using, and return to the oven for 2 minutes, or until melted.

OVEN-ROASTED ONIONS

Most people think of onions as an accompaniment to soups and casseroles, but they can be used as a stand-alone vegetable dish. Plus, they are good Candida killers. You will be pleased with the sweetness of these onions.

INGREDIENTS:

2 large sweet yellow onions
2 tablespoon coconut oil
1½ tablespoon balsamic vinegar

DIRECTIONS:

1. Preheat oven to 400° F.
2. Cut onions into 8 wedges each and place in a 9 by 13-inch glass pan.
3. In a small bowl, melt the oil and combine with the vinegar.
4. Toss the oil mixture over the onions.
5. Roast the onions in oven for 35 minutes.

BUTTERY GARLIC SPAGHETTI SQUASH

Serving plain spaghetti squash is a great replacement for noodles or rice. But if you want it as a side dish, flavor it up this way. I love this as a snack on winter evenings, too! There is just something comforting about garlic and that "buttery" flavor.

INGREDIENTS:

1 (1½- to 2-pound) spaghetti squash
4 tablespoons dairy- and soy-free margarine
½ tablespoon dried minced onion
¾ teaspoon minced garlic
½ teaspoon dried parsley

DIRECTIONS:

1. Preheat oven to 350° F.
2. Cut squash open lengthwise and gently scoop out seeds.
3. Place in a 9 by 13-inch glass baking dish
4. Pour about ½ inch of water into pan and cover it with foil
5. Bake for 40 to 45 minutes, or until squash pulls away from sides easily.
6. In a large skillet, melt the margarine over medium-low heat.
7. Add onion, garlic, and parsley to the margarine.
8. Use a fork to scrape out the squash.
9. Turn the heat to low and stir the squash into the margarine mixture.
10. Stir squash to coat.

BAKED SWEET POTATOES AND APPLES

This recipe first appeared on the blog as Grilled Sweet Potatoes and Apples. I have adapted the recipe to be more specific, and for the oven on those winter nights when firing up the grill isn't an option.

INGREDIENTS:

2 large sweet potatoes, peeled and cubed

2 large apples, peeled and cubed (pieces should be larger than the sweet potatoes)

2 tablespoons coconut oil

1 tablespoon coconut sugar

¼ teaspoon cinnamon

DIRECTIONS:

1. Preheat oven to 450° F.
2. In a 2-quart casserole dish, combine the sweet potatoes and apples.
3. In a separate bowl, melt the oil and stir in sugar and cinnamon.
4. Coat sweet potatoes with oil mixture.
5. Place a lid on the casserole dish and bake for 25 minutes, or until sweet potatoes are tender.

ONION AND GARLICKY MASHED CAULIFLOWER

This may take some work on your part, but I promise it will be hard to tell you are eating cauliflower. Use with any meal you would normally use mashed potatoes, or simply as a side dish.

INGREDIENTS:

2 tablespoons dairy- and soy-free margarine
1 onion, cut into small wedges
½ teaspoon minced garlic
1 head cauliflower, cut into florets
½ teaspoon salt
¼ teaspoon pepper
½ cup vegetable broth
½ cup mashed potato flakes (or more as needed)
Dried parsley for garnish, optional

DIRECTIONS:

1. In a skillet, melt margarine over medium heat.
2. Sauté onion and garlic for 6 to 7 minutes. Set aside.
3. Bring a large pot of water to a boil.
4. Add the cauliflower and boil for 10 to 15 minutes, or until easily pierced with a fork.
5. Drain cauliflower well.
6. Place onion, garlic, salt, and pepper into a large food processor.
7. Add cooked cauliflower and pulse several times.
8. Add broth and process until "mashed" well.
9. Add dry mashed potato flakes and pulse until combined. Add more, if necessary to get the desired consistency.
10. Sprinkle with dried parsley on top, if using.

COLLARD GREENS

Everyone is told to eat more leafy greens, but many don't know how. After all, you can eat only so many salads. Well, here is a great way to eat those leafy greens. And if you think you don't like collards, you might be surprised. Cooked this way, they are very good.

INGREDIENTS:

1 bunch collard greens
1 teaspoon minced garlic
2 tablespoons dairy- and soy-free margarine
1 teaspoon bottled lemon juice

DIRECTIONS:

1. Using a knife and a cutting board, remove the stems and center ribs from the collards.
2. Stack a few leaves at a time and cut into 1-inch squares.
3. Place leaves in a large pot and cover with water.
4. Bring to a boil and boil for 7 minutes.
5. Drain in a colander. Use a spoon to press the collards against the sides of the colander to get as much water out as possible.
6. Dry the pot with a paper towel.
7. Return pot to stove and add garlic, margarine, and lemon juice.
8. When the margarine is melted, add the leaves and stir to combine. Cook and stir for 4 to 5 minutes.
9. Serve immediately.

PEAS WITH GARLIC ONION BUTTER SAUCE

I like anything garlic and onion—they make everything better.
And they make peas just a little more exciting with this easy recipe.

INGREDIENTS:

2 cups frozen peas
2 tablespoons dairy- and soy-free margarine, melted
½ teaspoon dried minced onion
¼ teaspoon garlic powder

DIRECTIONS:

1. Cook peas in a glass covered dish in the microwave to the desired tenderness.
2. Drain well and set aside.
3. In the same dish, melt the margarine in the microwave and add the onion and garlic powder.
4. Return peas to the pan and stir to coat well.

ROASTED CAULIFLOWER

No need for a sauce to drench your cauliflower!
Roasting brings out a mild and sweet flavor that even kids will like.

INGREDIENTS:

1 large head of cauliflower
¼ cup olive oil
2 tablespoons bottled lemon juice
1 teaspoon minced garlic
¼ teaspoon pepper

DIRECTIONS:

1. Preheat oven to 400° F.
2. Wash cauliflower and cut into florets.
3. Place in a single layer in a 9 by 13-inch glass pan.
4. Mix the oil, lemon juice, garlic, and pepper and toss over the cauliflower to coat all pieces.
5. Roast in oven for 25 to 30 minutes, or until tender.

SAUTÉED KALE AND ONIONS

A few years ago, kale had its shining moment. It was touted as a superfood and was suddenly all over the blogosphere. Because it's not people's first choice as a vegetable for their meal, kale often gets completely looked over. But in addition to providing a nice variety to the table, it is a great source of antioxidants.

INGREDIENTS:

1 large onion, sliced
2 tablespoons coconut oil
1½ teaspoons minced garlic
1 head kale, washed and torn into pieces
¾ cup vegetable broth

DIRECTIONS:

1. In a skillet pan, heat oil over medium-high heat.
2. Add onion slices and cook and stir for about 5 minutes.
3. Add garlic and cook and stir for an additional 2 minutes.
4. Reduce heat to low and cook the onions another 5 minutes, or until brown and soft.
5. Add kale to the pan and return the heat to medium-high. (The pan will seem too full, but just wait—it will shrink fast.)
6. Add broth and cook and stir for 3 to 4 minutes, until the broth is absorbed and the kale is wilted.
7. Serve immediately.

ROASTED COLORED PEPPERS

I'm a huge fan of roasting vegetables at a high temperature. These peppers turn out sweet and succulent. This is so easy to prepare, you can hardly call it a recipe. Not to mention, it adds fun color to your dinner plate.

INGREDIENTS:

1 red bell pepper
1 orange bell pepper
1 yellow bell pepper
1 to 2 tablespoons grapeseed oil
Garlic powder (optional)

DIRECTIONS:

1. Preheat oven to 425° F.
2. Wash peppers, cut them open, and remove the seeds.
3. Slice each pepper into strips.
4. Place in a 9 by 13-inch glass pan and toss with oil.
5. Sprinkle with garlic powder, if using.
6. Roast in oven for 15 to 20 minutes.
7. Serve immediately.

EASY AND TASTY BRUSSEL SPROUTS

Brussel sprouts often get a bad rap. But they are basically mini cabbages boasting a lot of vitamins A, C, and Beta Carotene and deserve a chance. One thing I learned about vegetables . . . anything can taste good if you cook it right. Follow this recipe to a T, and I don't think you will be disappointed.

INGREDIENTS:

1 bag of frozen baby Brussel sprouts
1 tablespoon coconut oil
½ cup vegetable broth

DIRECTIONS:

1. Thaw Brussel sprouts.
2. If using regular Brussel sprouts (instead of baby ones), cut the large ones in half.
3. Heat oil in a skillet pan over medium heat.
4. Add sprouts and cook and stir for 5 to 6 minutes.
5. Add vegetable broth and bring to a simmer.
6. Reduce heat to medium-low, cover with a lid, and cook until sprouts are desired tenderness.

LEMON GARLIC BROCCOLI

There's nothing like a little lemon juice and garlic to really perk up vegetables. And the lemon juice helps to activate digestive enzymes, making vegetables easier to break down.

INGREDIENTS:

1 pound fresh broccoli
2 tablespoons olive oil
1 tablespoon bottled lemon juice
½ teaspoon minced garlic
Dash of salt and pepper

DIRECTIONS:

1. Cut broccoli into florets, wash, and drain in colander.
2. Place in a 2-quart casserole dish with a lid.
3. Add a little water to the bottom of pan.
4. Microwave on high for 5 to 6 minutes.
5. In a small bowl, combine the remaining ingredients.
6. Drain the broccoli and toss with the lemon and oil mixture.
7. Serve immediately.

OVEN BAKED GREEN BEANS

*There's nothing like fresh green beans in the summer, boiled on the stovetop
and served with a little melted margarine. Boy, that is good!
In the winter, I love them baked!*

INGREDIENTS:

1 pound fresh green beans
1 tablespoon grapeseed oil
¾ teaspoon garlic salt

DIRECTIONS:

1. Preheat oven to 400° F and line cookie sheet with parchment paper.
2. Wash beans and drain in colander.
3. Lay beans on cloth napkin, cover with cloth napkin, and pat to dry.
4. Snap ends off beans and place in bowl.
5. Toss with oil and garlic salt.
6. Place in a single layer on cookie sheet.
7. Bake for 20 to 22 minutes.

SCALLOPED POTATOES

Great for a holiday dinner yet easy enough for any time of the year, this recipe will knock your socks off.

INGREDIENTS:

5 large russet potatoes
3 tablespoons dairy- and soy-free margarine
1 onion, chopped
3 tablespoons garbanzo and fava bean flour (or sorghum flour)
1 teaspoon salt
¼ teaspoon pepper
1½ cups chicken broth
¼ cup Earth Balance Mindful Mayo
Paprika

DIRECTIONS:

1. Preheat oven to 350° F.
2. Spray a 9 by 13-inch glass pan lightly with cooking spray.
3. Scrub and peel the potatoes. Slice into thin slices and layer evenly in the pan.
4. In a large saucepan, melt margarine over medium heat.
5. Add onion and cook and stir for 5 minutes.
6. Add flour, salt, pepper, and broth. Stir until thick and bubbly.
7. Remove from heat.
8. Add the Mindful Mayo and stir to combine well.
9. Pour the mixture over the potatoes.
10. Sprinkle paprika evenly over the top of the potatoes.
11. Cover with foil and bake for 70 minutes.
12. Remove foil and bake for an additional 20 minutes.
13. Serve and enjoy immensely.

SEVEN WAYS TO FLAVOR RICE

Rice is a popular gluten-free grain, but it can get boring quickly if you eat it a lot. Here are seven recipes for making rice with some pizazz!

BROTH RICE:
Cook one cup brown rice in two cups chicken, vegetable, or beef broth according to package directions.

JERK RICE:
Cook one cup brown rice in one cup water, one cup chicken broth, and one teaspoon jerk seasoning according to package directions.

SALSA RICE:
Cook one cup brown rice in one cup water and one cup mild salsa according to package directions. (If you like, kick it up a notch with medium or hot salsa.)

SPICY BARBEQUE RICE:
Cook one cup brown rice in 1½ cups water and ½ cup spicy barbeque sauce according to package directions.

TERIYAKI RICE:
Get out a two-cup liquid measuring cup. In it, place 2 tablespoons olive oil, 2 tablespoons coconut aminos, 1 tablespoon ketchup, ½ tablespoon apple cider vinegar, ½ teaspoon garlic, and a dash of pepper. Add enough water to equal 2 cups. Cook with one cup brown rice according to package directions.

APPLE CINNAMON RAISIN RICE:
Cook one cup brown rice in one cup water, 1 cup apple juice, and ½ teaspoon of cinnamon according to package directions. When finished cooking, stir in 6 tablespoons dark raisins.

ITALIAN RICE:
Cook one cup brown rice in 1 cup water, 1 cup Italian Salad Dressing, ½ teaspoon dried basil, ½ teaspoon dried oregano, and ¼ teaspoon dried parsley according to package directions.

SWEET TREATS

From pies and cakes, to muffins, quick breads, and cookies, I've got you covered! These are the recipes you are looking for with the most traditional flavors in gluten-free, dairy-free, allergy-friendly baked goods that have no refined sugars.

It is important to note that substitutions to the flours or flour blends cannot be made in these recipes. Gluten-free flours and flour blends are not created equal and cannot be used interchangeably. So if I use Bob's, you use Bob's. If I use King Arthur, you use King Arthur. . .you get the idea. I've chosen these flour blends or flours because of their performance and because they are widely available. For those of you who are leery of Bob's Red Mill All Purpose Gluten Free Flour Blend, please don't be. If Bob's is good enough for Erin McKenna of Erin McKenna's Bakery (formally known as Babycakes), it is good enough for me. The same goes for starches: they are not interchangeable in baked goods. I know the tricks to making everything taste great. I use Bob's Red Mill for all my individual flours, except for buckwheat; for that, I use Arrowhead Mills.

I've also created the recipes around the weight of the flours, then converted them to measuring cups because most people don't want to weigh their flours. To get best results, you need to measure by using a spoon to fill your measuring cup, then leveling it off. No packing or scooping your cups!

For xanthan gum, I use Bob's Red Mill and find it to be the best and most trustworthy brand. Don't skip the gum. . .you'll be sorry. I know it's expensive, but it goes a long way. And it is highly important for the structure of your baked good.

I made most of the recipes egg free. For the few that do contain eggs, there is a good reason. Make them egg free at your own risk!

Milk and butter can be used in place of dairy-free milks and dairy-free, soy-free margarine in equal measurements; but the recipes have not been tested that way. Regular shortening can be used in place of palm oil shortening, but then your recipe won't be soy free! White sugar can be used in equal parts in any recipe to replace the xylitol or erythritol. (Please don't replace the coconut sugar—you'll change the flavor of the recipe.) If you replace the xylitol with sugar, your recipe will no longer be sugar free.

If not eaten the same day as they are baked, these treats should be frozen with the exception of pies and crisps.

Out of all the recipes in this book, these are the most important to follow to a T to make them work. But they all work, have been heavily tested, and taste great. No one will know they are gluten free or allergy friendly.

SINGLE PIE CRUST

I took several years figuring out this pie crust. So many gluten-free pie crust recipes are either way too lengthy or too difficult or simply taste bad. This one is easy and tastes great! The key is to start with really cold ingredients. It can be doubled for a two-crust pie.

INGREDIENTS:

1 cup King Arthur Gluten Free All-Purpose Flour
⅓ cup + 2 tablespoons palm oil shortening
2½ tablespoons water
1 tablespoon apple cider vinegar
¾ teaspoon xanthan gum

DIRECTIONS:

1. If you don't store your flour in the freezer (you should!), measure out the flour and place it in the freezer for 60 minutes.
2. Measure out shortening and place in freezer for 15 minutes.
3. Measure out water into a small plastic bowl and place in freezer for about 10 minutes.
4. In a food processor bowl, place the cold flour, shortening, water, vinegar, and gum.
5. Pulse 3 to 4 times and then run until the dough becomes a ball. It should form a ball really quickly. If it doesn't, the recipe won't work and you will need to start over.
6. Remove the ball of dough from the food processor and add any crumb mixture left in the bowl to the ball.
7. Place the ball of dough on a piece of parchment paper and flatten with your hands.
8. Cover with another piece of parchment paper and roll out to fit a 9-inch pie plate.
9. If you're baking the crust to fill later, bake at 475° F for about 8 minutes. Otherwise, bake according to the pie recipe instructions.

PUMPKIN PIE

I consider this pie recipe to be one of my crowning achievements. To make a pumpkin pie without eggs, milk, and soy (tofu), which was also free of refined sugars, seemed out of reach. But not anymore! This pumpkin pie recipe will soon be your favorite.

INGREDIENTS:

1 Single Pie Crust (page 97)
1 (13- to 14-ounce) can unsweetened, full-fat coconut milk
   (chilled for 48 hours)
¼ cup xylitol
½ cup coconut sugar
½ teaspoon vanilla
¼ teaspoon salt
1 teaspoon cinnamon
½ teaspoon ginger
½ teaspoon nutmeg
¼ teaspoon cloves
1 (15-ounce) can pumpkin puree
1 tablespoon unflavored gelatin
½ cup + 2 tablespoons unsweetened coconut milk (from a carton)

DIRECTIONS:

1. Make the pie crust in a 9-inch pie plate.
2. Preheat oven to 425° F.
3. In a large, high-speed blender, place all the remaining ingredients, run until combined, and scraping sides as necessary.
4. Pour the blender mixture into pie crust and smooth out the top.
5. Cover the pie crust edges with aluminum foil all the way around. (It usually takes 3 strips of foil.)
6. Bake for 15 minutes.
7. Reduce heat to 350° F and bake for another hour.
8. Let the pie cool on a cooling rack on the counter for 5 to 6 hours.
9. Place in refrigerator and cool for about 2 hours before serving.

FRENCH APPLE PIE

Apple pies might be a bit of work, but they are worth it. This single-crust pie (sometimes called Dutch Apple Pie) with unrefined sugars will blow your mind!

INGREDIENTS:

1 Single pie crust (page 97)

4 large Granny Smith apples, peeled, cored, and sliced

2 tablespoons sorghum flour (or brown rice flour)

⅓ cup + 2 tablespoons coconut nectar (a liquid similar to maple syrup)

2 tablespoons bottled lemon juice

TOPPING:

½ cup sorghum flour (or brown rice flour)

¼ cup tapioca starch

¼ cup golden flax meal

¼ cup coconut sugar

½ teaspoon cinnamon

6 tablespoons dairy- and soy-free margarine

DIRECTIONS:

1. Make the pie crust in a 9-inch pie plate.
2. Preheat oven to 425° F.
3. In a large bowl, combine apples, 2 tablespoons of the flour, coconut nectar, and lemon juice.
4. In another bowl, combine the dry topping ingredients.
5. Using a pastry cutter, add the margarine to the topping mixture until pea-sized crumbs are formed.
6. Place the apples in the pie crust.
7. Top the apples with the crumb mixture.
8. Using 3 strips of aluminum foil, cover the pie crust edges.
9. Place in oven and place a pizza pan on the rack below to catch any possible drips.
10. Bake for 20 minutes.
11. Gently place a flat sheet of aluminum foil over top of pie.
12. Bake for an additional 30 minutes.
13. Remove from the oven and, if possible, wait 7 to 8 hours before cutting.

CHERRY CRISP

I love crisps since they are so easy to make. This one often debuts at my Thanksgiving table along with a pumpkin pie.

INGREDIENTS:

2 (14- to 15-ounce) cans of cherries in water
½ cup maple syrup
1½ tablespoons bottled lemon juice
¼ cup quick-cooking tapioca pearls

TOPPING:

¼ cup sorghum flour (or brown rice flour)
1½ cups gluten-free rolled oats
¼ cup golden flax meal
⅓ cup coconut sugar
¼ cup + 2 tablespoons canola oil

DIRECTIONS:

1. Preheat oven to 375° F.
2. Drain cherries well.
3. In a bowl, combine cherries, syrup, lemon juice, and tapioca pearls.
4. Let it sit for about 5 minutes.
5. In another bowl, combine the topping ingredients.
6. Spray an 8 by 8-inch pan with cooking spray.
7. Place cherry mixture in the pan.
8. Pour oil into the topping mixture and stir to make a "damp" consistency.
9. Spread the oat mixture evenly over the cherries.
10. Bake for 30 minutes.

APPLE CRANBERRY CRISP

Stock up on cranberries around Thanksgiving when they are cheap and keep them in the freezer for use at any time. The combination of apples with the cranberries will diminish any tartness.

INGREDIENTS:

3 cups peeled, chopped apples
2 cups cranberries, fresh or frozen
½ cup xylitol
1 tablespoon coconut nectar
3 tablespoons sorghum flour (or brown rice flour)

TOPPING:

1½ cups gluten-free rolled oats
¼ cup sorghum flour (or brown rice flour)
¼ cup golden flax meal
⅓ cup coconut sugar
¼ cup + 2 tablespoons canola oil

DIRECTIONS:

1. Preheat oven to 350° F.
2. In a bowl, combine apples, cranberries, xylitol, coconut nectar, and 3 tablespoons of the sorghum flour.
3. In a separate bowl, combine all the topping ingredients, except the oil.
4. Spray 8 by 8-inch baking pan with cooking spray.
5. Place fruit mixture in the pan and spread evenly.
6. Spread the topping mixture on top of the fruit.
7. Pour oil over the top evenly.
8. Bake for 50 minutes.

ZUCCHINI BREAD

I wanted a zucchini bread that tasted just like the one I grew up with, but without all the gluten and sugar, so I came up with this recipe. This is one of the few recipes in the book that uses eggs. I also use mini loaf pans (3 by 5 ½ inch), which I highly recommend.

INGREDIENTS:

1¾ cups Bob's Red Mill Gluten Free All Purpose Baking Flour
¼ teaspoon salt
¼ teaspoon nutmeg
¼ teaspoon cinnamon
1 teaspoon baking powder
1½ teaspoons xanthan gum
2 eggs
¼ cup + 2 tablespoons coconut oil, melted
2 tablespoons canola oil
½ cup coconut sugar
½ teaspoon liquid stevia
1 teaspoon vanilla
1 cup grated zucchini

DIRECTIONS:

1. Preheat oven to 350° F.
2. In a large bowl, combine the flour, salt, nutmeg, cinnamon, baking powder, and gum.
3. In another bowl, combine the eggs, both oils, sugar, stevia, vanilla, and zucchini.
4. Pour the wet ingredients into the dry. Stir until well combined, making sure to incorporate all the dry ingredients.
5. Spray two mini loaf pans with cooking spray.
6. Divide the batter evenly between the two pans.
7. Bake for 35 minutes, or until inserted toothpick comes out clean.
8. Remove from pans and cool on a cooling rack.

CRANBERRY ORANGE BREAD

While this may seem like a holiday bread, I like it year round.
It's the perfect combination of sweet and tart!

INGREDIENTS:

1¾ cups + 1 tablespoon Bob's Red Mill Gluten Free
    All Purpose Baking Flour
½ cup coconut sugar
¼ cup xylitol
2 teaspoons baking powder
1½ teaspoons xanthan gum
¾ teaspoon salt
½ teaspoon baking soda
1 cup cranberries, chopped (make sure they are dry after washing)
¼ cup unsweetened applesauce
½ teaspoon vanilla
2 tablespoons coconut oil, melted
⅔ cup orange juice

DIRECTIONS:

1. Preheat oven to 350° F.
2. In a large bowl, combine the first 7 ingredients. Whisk well.
3. Add the cranberries, applesauce, vanilla, and coconut oil. Stir.
4. Add the orange juice last.
5. Stir to combine. Pour the batter into 3 small bread pans (3 by 5½ inches) that have been sprayed with cooking spray.
6. Bake for 35 minutes, or until inserted toothpick comes out clean.
7. Remove from pans and cool on a cooling rack.

BUCKWHEAT CHIA BANANA MUFFINS

Pack this healthy, low-sugar muffin in a lunch as a sandwich replacement or serve for breakfast or snack.

INGREDIENTS:

¾ cup buckwheat flour
2 tablespoons potato starch
2 tablespoons tapioca starch
2 tablespoons chia seeds
3 teaspoons baking powder
¼ teaspoon salt
¾ teaspoon xanthan gum
2 tablespoons xylitol
2 tablespoons coconut sugar
1 teaspoon cinnamon
1 teaspoon vanilla
1½ cups mashed banana

DIRECTIONS:

1. Preheat oven to 350° F and line 12 muffin tins with paper liners.
2. In a large bowl, combine all the ingredients except vanilla and banana.
3. In a separate bowl, combine the vanilla and banana.
4. Add the banana to the dry ingredients, making sure to incorporate all dry ingredients.
5. Bake for 14 minutes, or until inserted toothpick comes out clean.
6. Remove muffins from pan and cool on cooling rack.

BANANA CHOCOLATE CHIP MUFFINS

Right out of the oven, these muffins ooze melted chocolate and taste decadent.

INGREDIENTS:

1¾ cups Bob's Red Mill Gluten Free All Purpose Baking Flour
½ teaspoon salt
2 teaspoons baking powder
1½ teaspoons xanthan gum
¼ teaspoon cinnamon
½ cup coconut sugar
½ cup mashed banana
¼ cup + 1 tablespoon coconut oil, melted
½ cup + 2 tablespoons unsweetened almond milk (or rice milk)
1 teaspoon vanilla
⅔ cup dairy-free, soy-free chocolate chips

DIRECTIONS:

1. Preheat oven to 400° F and line 12 muffin tins with paper liners.
2. Combine the first 6 ingredients in a large bowl and whisk together.
3. Add the mashed banana, oil, milk, and vanilla. Stir to combine.
4. Add the chocolate chips and stir to combine.
5. Distribute the batter among the 12 muffin tins.
6. Bake for 14 minutes.
7. Remove muffins from pan and cool on cooling rack.

APPLE CINNAMON MUFFINS

Everyone needs a basic apple muffin recipe. Here you go.

INGREDIENTS:

1¾ cup + 1 tablespoon Bob's Red Mill Gluten Free All Purpose Baking Flour
¼ cup xylitol
¼ cup coconut sugar
3 teaspoons baking powder
½ teaspoon salt
1½ teaspoons xanthan gum
1 teaspoon cinnamon
¼ teaspoon nutmeg
¼ cup unsweetened applesauce
¼ cup coconut oil
¾ cup unsweetened coconut or almond milk
1¼ cups chopped, peeled apple

DIRECTIONS:

1. Preheat oven to 400° F and line 12 muffin tins with paper liners.
2. In a large bowl, combine the first 8 ingredients.
3. In a small microwaveable bowl, combine applesauce and oil.
4. Heat on power 2 for 1 to 2 minutes, until oil is melted.
5. Add applesauce and oil mixture to dry ingredients.
6. Add milk and apple.
7. Stir to combine, making sure to incorporate all dry ingredients.
8. Place batter into muffin tins and bake for 20 minutes.
9. Remove muffins from pan and cool on cooling rack.

APPLE CINNAMON CAKE

*A simple, yet delicious cake, great for harvest time or any time of the year.
This is one of the few recipes that call for eggs.*

INGREDIENTS:

2 cups Bob's Red Mill Gluten Free All Purpose Baking Flour
1 teaspoon cinnamon
1 teaspoon baking powder
1 teaspoon xanthan gum
½ teaspoon salt
½ cup xylitol
¼ cup coconut sugar
1 cup canola oil
⅔ teaspoon liquid stevia
2 eggs
4 cups (about 3 large) peeled, chopped Granny Smith apples

DIRECTIONS:

1. Preheat oven to 350° F.
2. In a large bowl, combine the first 7 ingredients. Whisk well.
3. Add the oil and stevia and stir briefly.
4. In a small bowl, slightly whisk the two eggs to break up the yolks.
5. Add to the cake batter and stir to thoroughly combine.
6. Add apples and stir to coat them all.
7. Spray an 8 by 8-inch baking pan with cooking spray.
8. Pour cake batter into the pan and spread evenly.
9. Bake for 45 minutes, or until inserted toothpick comes out clean.

CHOCOLATE CAKE

Every gluten-free, allergy-friendly cookbook needs a chocolate cake recipe. This one-layer chocolate cake tastes more fudgy than cakey and works well with the Sugar-Free Vanilla Frosting on page 109. Perfect for birthday celebrations or anytime you crave chocolate.

INGREDIENTS:

¾ cup + 3 tablespoons Bob's Red Mill Gluten Free All Purpose
    Baking Flour
¼ cup xylitol
½ cup coconut sugar
½ cup cocoa powder
2 teaspoons baking powder
¾ teaspoon baking soda
½ teaspoon salt
½ teaspoon xanthan gum
¼ cup unsweetened applesauce
½ cup unsweetened coconut milk
¼ cup canola oil
2 teaspoons vanilla
¼ teaspoon liquid stevia
½ cup very hot tap water
1 teaspoon apple cider vinegar
Sugar Free Vanilla Frosting (page 109, optional)

DIRECTIONS:

1. Preheat oven to 325° F.
2. Spray the sides and bottom of an 8 by 8-inch metal baking pan with cooking spray.
3. In a large bowl, combine the first 8 ingredients. Whisk well.
4. Add the applesauce, milk, oil, vanilla, and stevia. Stir to combine.
5. Add hot water and stir.
6. Add the apple cider vinegar last and stir.
7. Pour batter into the prepared pan and immediately place in the oven.
8. Bake for 40 minutes, or until inserted toothpick comes out clean.

SUGAR-FREE VANILLA FROSTING

This sugar-free vanilla frosting tastes and acts the same as the kind chock-full of sugar. It makes enough for a thin layer on an 8 by 8-inch cake. It is very important to use erythritol and not xylitol in this recipe. Feel free to double or triple it if you need more.

INGREDIENTS:

½ cup erythritol
¼ cup arrowroot powder
¼ cup coconut milk powder
2 teaspoons vanilla
2½ tablespoons dairy- and soy-free margarine
⅓ teaspoon liquid stevia

DIRECTIONS:

1. In a high-speed blender, place the erythritol and arrowroot powder.
2. Pulse 5 times and then run on high for 30 seconds.
3. Remove the container from the blender base and shake well.
4. Add the coconut milk powder to the erythritol and arrowroot, return the blender to the base, and run on high for 30 seconds.
5. Shake well and place in a bowl.
6. Add the vanilla, margarine, and stevia to the bowl and use an electric mixer to beat into a creamy frosting.

CHOCOLATE CHIP COOKIE CAKE

A staple of classroom birthday treats, this chocolate chip cookie cake is simple and simply delicious! And I dare say . . . better than its wheat-filled counterpart!

INGREDIENTS:

½ cup (8 tablespoons) dairy- and soy-free margarine
¼ cup xylitol
¼ cup coconut sugar
¼ cup unsweetened applesauce
1 teaspoon vanilla
1 teaspoon baking powder
1¼ teaspoons xanthan gum
¼ teaspoon salt
1⅓ cups King Arthur Gluten Free All-Purpose Flour
⅔ cup dairy- and soy-free chocolate chips

DIRECTIONS:

1. Preheat oven to 350° F and spray the sides and bottom of a 9-inch round baking pan.
2. In a mixer bowl, combine the margarine, xylitol, and sugar until slightly creamed.
3. Add applesauce and vanilla and beat another 1 to 2 minutes. Add baking powder, gum, salt, and flour.
4. Remove bowl from the mixer.
5. Spray your hands with cooking spray.
6. Using your hands, mix the dough thoroughly until a ball forms.
7. Add chocolate chips (re-spray hands, if needed) and incorporate into dough.
8. Place batter in the prepared pan and evenly spread the dough to the sides.
9. Bake for 20 to 22 minutes. Remove from the oven.
10. Rest in pan for about 8 minutes and then invert cookie cake onto a cooling rack.
11. Cool before cutting into wedges.

CINNAMON RAISIN MUG CAKE

Mugs cakes are single serve desserts that bake fast and are perfect for anyone! I love this simple mug cake because I love anything raisin. This could even work for breakfast; just mix the dry ingredients the night before to speed up the process in the morning.

INGREDIENTS:

1 tablespoon canola oil
3 tablespoons unsweetened applesauce
1 tablespoon unsweetened almond or coconut milk
1 tablespoon xylitol
1 tablespoon coconut sugar
2 tablespoons sorghum flour
½ tablespoon potato starch
⅛ teaspoon vanilla
½ teaspoon cinnamon
¼ teaspoon baking powder
2 tablespoons raisins

DIRECTIONS:

1. In a small bowl, mix all the ingredients (except raisins) until all dry ingredients are incorporated.
2. Add raisins and stir.
3. Place batter in a mug and microwave for 3 minutes to 3 minutes and 15 seconds.
4. Let cool for about 5 minutes and then enjoy warm straight from the mug.

DOUBLE CHOCOLATE MUG CAKE

Want a piece of chocolate cake after a long day?
Now you can have one in a few short minutes!

INGREDIENTS:

1 tablespoon canola oil

3 tablespoons unsweetened applesauce

1½ tablespoons unsweetened almond or coconut milk

2 tablespoons xylitol

2 tablespoons sorghum flour

½ tablespoon potato starch

2 tablespoons cocoa powder

¼ teaspoon baking powder

⅛ teaspoon vanilla

2 tablespoons dairy- and soy-free chocolate chips

DIRECTIONS:

1. In a small bowl, mix all the ingredients (except chocolate chips) until all dry ingredients are incorporated.
2. Add chocolate chips and stir to combine.
3. Place batter in a mug and microwave for 3 minutes to 3 minutes and 15 seconds.
4. Let cool for about 5 minutes and then enjoy warm straight from the mug.

NUTTY CHOCOLATE CHIP MUG CAKE

If I make a full-sized cake, I'll eat a whole cake. This is the perfect remedy . . .
a single piece of cake in just a few short minutes.

INGREDIENTS:

1 tablespoon unsweetened cashew butter (or almond or peanut butter)
3 tablespoons unsweetened applesauce
1 tablespoon unsweetened almond or coconut milk
1 tablespoon xylitol
1 tablespoon coconut sugar
2 tablespoons sorghum flour
½ tablespoon potato starch
⅛ teaspoon vanilla
¼ teaspoon baking powder
2 tablespoons dairy- and soy-free chocolate chips

DIRECTIONS:

1. In a small bowl, mix all the ingredients (except chocolate chips) until all dry ingredients are incorporated.
2. Add chocolate chips and stir to combine.
3. Place batter in a mug and microwave for 3 minutes to 3 minutes 15 seconds.
4. Let cool for about 5 minutes and then enjoy warm straight from the mug.

PINEAPPLE UPSIDE-DOWN CAKE

Pineapple Upside-Down Cake doesn't have to be tricky or full of sugar.
This cake has no refined sugars, is simple to make, and is pretty to look at.

INGREDIENTS:

1½ tablespoons coconut oil
3 tablespoons coconut sugar
8 pineapple rings, drained
2 tablespoons palm oil shortening
¼ cup xylitol
½ teaspoon liquid stevia
¼ cup unsweetened applesauce
⅓ cup unsweetened coconut milk
½ teaspoon vanilla
1¼ cups Bob's Red Mill Gluten Free All Purpose Baking Flour
2½ teaspoons baking powder
½ teaspoon xanthan gum
¼ teaspoon salt

DIRECTIONS:

1. Preheat oven to 350° F and spray a 9-inch round cake pan with cooking spray.
2. Melt coconut oil and stir in the coconut sugar.
3. Spread the sugar and oil mixture in the pan. (It won't cover the whole bottom.)
4. Place 7 pineapple rings on top of the sugar mixture. Break up the 8th ring to fill in gaps along the edge of the pan.
5. In a large bowl, cream shortening, xylitol, stevia, applesauce, milk, and vanilla.
6. In a separate bowl, combine the flour, baking powder, gum, and salt.
7. Pour dry ingredients into wet ingredients and stir to combine well, making sure to incorporate all the dry flour.
8. Spread over the pineapple rings.
9. Bake for 20 minutes or until an inserted toothpick comes out clean.
10. Rest in pan for 10 minutes before inverting onto a cooling rack.

SOFT ALLERGY-FREE CHOCOLATE CHIP COOKIES

A remake from the blog, this cookie is sure to delight anyone!

INGREDIENTS:

1 cup King Arthur Gluten Free All-Purpose Flour
1 tablespoon potato starch
¼ teaspoon xanthan gum
2 teaspoons baking powder
½ teaspoon salt
½ teaspoon vanilla
½ cup palm oil shortening
¼ cup coconut nectar or maple syrup
¼ cup applesauce
¼ teaspoon liquid stevia
½ cup dairy- and soy-free chocolate chips

DIRECTIONS:

1. Preheat oven to 350° F.
2. In a large bowl, combine the first 5 ingredients.
3. In another bowl, combine the vanilla, shortening, coconut nectar, applesauce, and stevia.
4. Add the wet mixture to the dry ingredients and stir until combined, making sure to incorporate all the dry ingredients.
5. Mix in the chocolate chips.
6. Line the cookie sheets with parchment paper.
7. Place the cookie dough by spoonfuls on the sheets and bake for 8 minutes.
8. Remove from the oven and let the cookies rest on the sheets for 1 minute before transferring to a cooling rack.

GRAIN-FREE CHOCOLATE CHIP COOKIES

You can indulge in these cookies guilt free. Made with almond meal and sweetened with stevia, these cookies nearly melt in your mouth. You will never be able to eat just one!

INGREDIENTS:

1¼ cups almond meal
¼ cup unsweetened applesauce
1 teaspoon baking powder
⅓ teaspoon liquid stevia
½ teaspoon vanilla
¼ teaspoon salt
3 tablespoons canola oil
¼ cup dairy- and soy-free chocolate chips

DIRECTIONS:

1. Preheat oven to 375° F and line a cookie sheet with parchment paper.
2. In a bowl, place all ingredients (except chocolate chips). Stir to combine.
3. Then fold the chocolate chips into the dough.
4. Place the cookie dough by spoonfuls onto the cookie sheets.
5. Bake for 7 minutes, and then remove to a cooling rack.

DOUBLE CHOCOLATE FUDGY COOKIES

Tell no one you put avocado in these cookies, and they will never know!
These seriously fudgy cookies are the perfect chocolate fix. And they're grain free!
(If you desire, sorghum flour does work in place of the garbanzo and fava bean flour,
but then they won't be grain free).

INGREDIENTS:

2 ripe avocados
½ teaspoon liquid stevia
½ cup coconut sugar
2 teaspoons vanilla
1 cup cocoa powder
2 tablespoons flax meal mixed with 6 tablespoons warm water
⅔ cup garbanzo and fava bean flour
½ cup unsweetened applesauce
2 teaspoons baking powder
¼ teaspoon xanthan gum
½ cup dairy- and soy-free chocolate chips

DIRECTIONS:

1. Preheat oven to 350° F and line cookie sheets with parchment paper.
2. Scoop out ripe avocados and place in a large food processor.
3. Add stevia, sugar, vanilla, and cocoa powder.
4. Process for about 1 minute.
5. Add the flax meal mixture, flour, applesauce, baking powder, and gum to the avocado mixture.
6. Process until smooth and without visible avocado chunks.
7. Remove blade and stir in the chocolate chips.
8. Place the cookie dough by spoonfuls onto the baking sheets.
9. Bake for 8 minutes.
10. Remove from the oven and place the cookies on a cooling rack.

PUMPKIN RAISIN COOKIES

*Light on pumpkin, these fluffy cookies, full of autumnal spices are
sure to hit the spot in the fall or any time of the year.*

INGREDIENTS:

½ cup palm oil shortening
¼ cup + 1 tablespoon unsweetened applesauce
½ teaspoon vanilla
½ cup canned pumpkin
¼ cup coconut sugar
¼ teaspoon liquid stevia
1 cup Bob's Red Mill Gluten Free All Purpose Baking Flour
1¼ teaspoons baking powder
¼ teaspoon salt
¼ teaspoon cloves
¼ teaspoon cinnamon
⅛ teaspoon nutmeg
¼ teaspoon xanthan gum
½ cup dark raisins

DIRECTIONS:

1. Preheat oven to 325° F and line cookie sheets with parchment paper.
2. In a bowl, cream together the first 6 ingredients.
3. In another bowl, combine the flour, baking powder, salt, spices, and gum.
4. Place wet ingredients into the bowl with the dry ingredients. Stir to combine, making sure to get all the dry pieces incorporated.
5. Add raisins and stir to evenly distribute.
6. Place cookies by spoonfuls on cookie sheets.
7. Bake for 10 minutes, and then remove to cooling rack.

GINGERBREAD COOKIES

*Crunchy Gingerbread Cookies made gluten, dairy, and allergy free!
Fast and easy, this recipe needs no xanthan gum.*

INGREDIENTS:

1 cup Bob's Red Mill Gluten Free All Purpose Baking Flour
½ teaspoon salt
¼ teaspoon baking powder
2 teaspoons cinnamon
½ teaspoon cloves
½ teaspoon dried powdered ginger
2 tablespoons canola oil
¼ cup pure maple syrup

DIRECTIONS:

1. Preheat oven to 375° F and line a cookie sheet with parchment paper.
2. Whisk together the dry ingredients.
3. Add the oil and maple syrup.
4. Mix, using hands if needed, to form a big ball.
5. Divide the ball of dough into 15 little balls.
6. Place the balls on a cookie sheet and press down on each cookie with the palm of your hand.
7. Bake for 8 to 10 minutes.
8. As soon as the cookies come out of the oven, flatten each with the backside of a spatula.
9. Transfer to a cooling rack and cool completely so they crisp up.

MOLASSES COOKIES

Similar to the Gingerbread cookies, these also don't need xanthan gum—and you can't stop at just one!

INGREDIENTS:

1 cup Bob's Red Mill Gluten Free All Purpose Baking Flour
½ teaspoon salt
¼ teaspoon baking powder
1 teaspoon cinnamon
⅓ teaspoon dried powdered ginger
1 tablespoon xylitol
2 tablespoons + 1 teaspoon canola oil
3 tablespoons mild molasses
1 tablespoon maple syrup

DIRECTIONS:

1. Preheat oven to 375° F and line a cookie sheet with parchment paper.
2. Whisk together the dry ingredients.
3. Add the oil, molasses, and maple syrup.
4. Mix, using hands if needed, to form a big ball.
5. Divide the ball of dough into 15 little balls.
6. Place balls on a cookie sheet and press down on each cookie with the palm of your hand.
7. Bake for 8 to 10 minutes.
8. As soon as the cookies come out of the oven, flatten each with the backside of a spatula.
9. Transfer to a cooling rack and cool completely so they crisp up.

RAISIN SPICE COOKIES

*I love anything with raisins in it, and I love cinnamon and nutmeg.
Cookies are one of the best places to find these flavors!*

INGREDIENTS:

1¼ cups + 2 tablespoons Bob's Red Mill Gluten Free All Purpose
    Baking Flour
1 teaspoon cinnamon
½ teaspoon allspice
½ teaspoon nutmeg
¼ teaspoon + ⅛ teaspoon xanthan gum
½ teaspoon baking soda
½ teaspoon baking powder
½ teaspoon salt
¼ cup xylitol
¼ cup coconut sugar
½ teaspoon liquid stevia
¼ cup unsweetened applesauce
1½ tablespoons unsweetened almond milk (or rice milk)
½ tablespoon apple cider vinegar
¼ teaspoon vanilla
½ cup coconut oil, melted
⅓ cup raisins

DIRECTIONS:

1. Preheat oven to 350° F and line cookie sheets with parchment paper.
2. In a large bowl, combine the dry ingredients. Whisk well.
3. Add the stevia, applesauce, milk, vinegar, and vanilla. Stir together well.
4. Add melted coconut oil and then add raisins. Stir until well combined.
5. Place the cookie dough by spoonfuls onto the cookie sheets.
6. Bake for 12 minutes and then remove to cooling rack.

BROWNIES

Making a gluten-free brownie that is also egg free has been elusive until now. After many attempts, I have found a gluten-free, egg-free chocolate brownie that is also low in sugar and fat but without compromising on flavor. If you are used to gobs of sugar these may take some getting used to.

INGREDIENTS:

1 tablespoon chia seeds

¼ cup water

¼ cup coconut oil

½ cup dairy- and soy-free chocolate chips

¼ cup unsweetened applesauce

¼ cup coconut sugar

¼ teaspoon liquid stevia

1 teaspoon vanilla

1 cup Bob's Red Mill Gluten Free All Purpose Baking Flour

1 teaspoon xanthan gum

2 teaspoons baking powder

DIRECTIONS:

1. Mix the chia seeds with water and let sit for at least 15 minutes.
2. Preheat oven to 350° F and coat an 8 by 8-inch pan with cooking spray
3. In a 3-quart saucepan, melt the oil and chocolate chips over medium-low heat.
4. Remove from the heat and add the applesauce, sugar, stevia, and vanilla, stirring after each addition.
5. Stir in the flour, gum, and baking powder.
6. Add the chia/water mixture and stir until combined.
7. Place batter in the 8 by 8-inch pan.
8. Bake for 20 minutes.
9. Cool completely before cutting into squares.

CHOCOLATE NUTTY PROTEIN BARS

Great for an after-workout protein boost or just a snack to get you through to supper, these no-bake protein bars come together fast. And they taste great, too. Bonus!

INGREDIENTS:

2 tablespoons flax meal

2 tablespoons sunflower seeds

¼ cup unsweetened cashew butter (or almond butter)

½ tablespoon vanilla

¼ cup 100% pure maple syrup

½ cup gluten-free rolled oats

½ cup chocolate pea protein powder

DIRECTIONS:

1. Get out a small glass pan, about 5 by 7 inches.
2. In a bowl, combine all ingredients.
3. Wet your hands with cold water, scoop up the mixture, and place into the pan.
4. Pat down the mixture and smooth it out with your hands, rewetting them if needed.
5. Cover and refrigerate for at least 4 hours before cutting.
6. Store in the refrigerator.

NO-BAKE BARS

Perfect for a warm day when you don't want to turn the oven on, these bars will satisfy your sweet tooth beyond your imagination.

INGREDIENTS:

2 tablespoons sunflower seeds
2 tablespoons raisins
2 tablespoons dried cranberries
2 tablespoons dairy- and soy-free chocolate chips
5 large Medjool dates
¼ cup gluten-free rolled oats
1¾ cups gluten-free puffed rice cereal
¼ cup honey
2 tablespoons coconut sugar
⅓ cup + 1 tablespoon unsweetened sunflower seed butter (or almond butter)
¼ cup powdered rice milk
¼ teaspoon vanilla

DIRECTIONS:

1. Place the first 5 ingredients listed in a food processor.
2. Pulse until the pieces are uniform in size.
3. In a large bowl, combine the ingredients from the food processor with the oats and puffed rice cereal.
4. In a small microwaveable bowl, combine the honey, coconut sugar, sunflower seed butter, powdered rice milk, and vanilla.
5. Microwave on high for 30 seconds. Stir and microwave another 20 seconds.
6. Pour onto the dry ingredients and stir until combined.
7. Spray an 8 by 6-inch glass pan with cooking spray as well as sheet of wax paper.
8. Place the mixture into the pan and use the wax paper with the spray side facing down to spread out the mixture evenly.
9. Wait at least 30 minutes before cutting.

MISCELLANEOUS RECIPES

In this section, you will find all my great recipes that do not particularly fall neatly into any of the other categories. But there are a few gems in here you won't want to miss, such as my sandwich bread, mashed potato biscuits, and my favorite eating chocolate!

SANDWICH BREAD

Necessity is the mother of invention. That couldn't be truer than with this bread recipe. I never intended to bake or make gluten-free bread for myself; but when a gluten-free diet became necessary for others in my family, then I needed to get creative. It is relatively easy (for gluten-free bread, anyway) and tastes close to wheat bread (if I remember correctly). It requires a special-sized loaf pan, has a tight crumb, and is the perfect balance—neither dense and rock hard, nor light and starchy.

INGREDIENTS:

1 cup sorghum flour

½ cup teff flour

½ cup potato starch

½ cup tapioca starch

2 teaspoons baking powder

4 tablespoons coconut sugar, divided

1 teaspoon salt

2 teaspoons xanthan gum

2 eggs

2 packets active dry yeast

¼ cup warm water (110° F)

⅓ cup grapeseed oil

½ cup club soda

DIRECTIONS:

1. In a large bowl, combine the flours, starches, baking powder, 3 tablespoons of the coconut sugar, salt, and gum.
2. Remove eggs and yeast from the refrigerator and set on the counter.
3. Let the dry ingredients in the bowl and the items on the counter warm up to room temperature for about 30 minutes.
4. Break the eggs into a small bowl and whisk until beaten well.
5. In another bowl, combine the 110° F water, the remaining 1 tablespoon of coconut sugar, and yeast. Whisk and then set aside until frothy, about 5 minutes.
6. To the flour mixture, add the eggs, oil, yeast mixture, and club soda.
7. Stir well to combine all dry ingredients, making sure to get all dry ingredients incorporated.
8. Spray the sides and bottom of a 4 by 8-inch bread pan with cooking spray.
9. Place batter in the pan and let it rise 10 to 30 minutes, until the batter is level with the top of the pan. (Time will be less on a warm day, more on a cooler day.)
10. While the batter is rising, preheat the oven to 375° F.
11. Bake for 20 minutes.
12. Cover loosely with aluminum foil and bake for an additional 25 minutes.
13. The bread is done when the internal temperature is 200° F.
14. Transfer from pan onto cooling rack immediately.
15. Cool completely before cutting.
16. To store, cut into slices, place wax paper squares between each slice, and freeze.
17. To serve, remove the pieces you need from the freezer and thaw.

MASHED POTATO BISCUITS

*These biscuits are so easy to whip up, and they go with just about anything!
They freeze well, too.*

INGREDIENTS:

1 cup Bob's Red Mill Gluten Free All Purpose Baking Flour
⅓ cup + 1 tablespoon dry mashed potato flakes
½ tablespoon baking powder
½ teaspoon salt
¼ teaspoon xanthan gum
3½ tablespoons dairy- and soy-free margarine, melted
⅓ cup + 1 tablespoon unsweetened almond or coconut milk
¼ cup water

DIRECTIONS:

1. Preheat oven to 425° F and line a cookie sheet with parchment paper.
2. In a large bowl, combine the first 5 ingredients.
3. Add the melted margarine, milk, and water. Stir well.
4. Spray the inside of a ¼-cup measuring cup with cooking spray and then wipe out with a paper towel.
5. Use this ¼ cup measuring cup to scoop out approximately six biscuits.
6. Bake for 12 minutes.

FAVORITE EATING CHOCOLATE

Everyone needs a little chocolate in their life! And this is the perfect way to consume the very healthy fat . . . coconut oil. And what's even better? It's free of dairy and refined sugars! Omit the raisins if you want plain eating chocolate.
(It won't be as sweet though!)

INGREDIENTS:

¼ cup + 1 tablespoon coconut oil
3 tablespoons palm oil shortening
½ cup cocoa powder
2 tablespoons honey
12 drops liquid stevia
¾ cup raisins (optional)

DIRECTIONS:

1. In a saucepan, melt the oil and shortening over low heat.
2. Add cocoa powder and stir to combine well.
3. Add honey and stevia and stir well several times.
4. Remove from heat.
5. Stir the raisins into the chocolate, if using.
6. Spray the bottom of a 5 by 7-inch glass pan with cooking spray.
7. Cut out a piece of parchment paper a little bigger than the bottom of the pan.
8. Press the paper onto the cooking spray. (This helps the paper stick.)
9. Pour chocolate into the pan and freeze for about 3 hours.
10. Remove from freezer and pull up on the parchment paper to remove the chocolate.
11. Place the chocolate bar on a cutting board.
12. Using a large chef knife, cut the chocolate into little squares.
13. Keep the squares on the cutting board and place in the freezer for about 10 minutes.
14. Remove from freezer and place the chocolate squares in a plastic container with a lid.
15. Store in the freezer.
16. Whenever you want a little bit of chocolate, remove one square and enjoy!

CANDIED PECANS

Like potato chips, you can't eat just one. But with the healthy fat, coconut oil, and low-glycemic coconut sugar and pecans . . . it's okay to indulge. I won't tell.

INGREDIENTS:

2 tablespoons coconut oil (or dairy- and soy-free margarine)
½ tablespoon water
6 tablespoons coconut sugar
1½ cups pecan halves

DIRECTIONS:

1. In a saucepan, melt oil on low heat.
2. Add the water and coconut sugar. Cook and stir until slightly thickened.
3. Remove from heat and add pecans.
4. Stir to coat evenly.
5. Place a piece of wax paper on the counter.
6. Spread the pecan halves on the wax paper to cool and harden.
7. If the room temperature is too warm, you may need to place them in the refrigerator to harden.
8. Then store in refrigerator in a container with a lid.

VANILLA GLAZE

*Here is a basic vanilla glaze for cut out cookies or a Bundt cake.
It makes a small amount, but packs big flavor!*

INGREDIENTS:

¼ cup erythritol

¼ cup arrowroot powder

½ teaspoon vanilla

2 tablespoons + 1 teaspoon unsweetened coconut milk

3 to 5 drops liquid stevia (optional)

DIRECTIONS:

1. Combine the erythritol and arrowroot powder in a high-speed blender (a food processor would not work) and process until it is a fine powder.
2. Place the contents in a small bowl.
3. Add milk and vanilla and stir to combine to right consistency. If needed, add a little more milk, but be careful. If it gets too thin, add a little arrowroot powder.
4. Stir in stevia drops to taste.
5. Spread on cooled, cut-out cookies or drizzle wherever you need a glaze.

CRANBERRY SAUCE

Next to pumpkin pie, cranberry sauce is one of my favorite Thanksgiving dishes. I know, I'm weird that way. I'm also a cranberry sauce snob, so please don't buy that canned stuff! It's chock-full of high fructose corn syrup and who knows what else. Making your own is not difficult, and it can be made several days in advance.

INGREDIENTS:

1 bag cranberries, washed and thawed if previously frozen
1 cup water
½ cup coconut sugar
½ teaspoon liquid stevia
1 tablespoon 100% pure maple syrup (optional)

DIRECTIONS:

1. Place cranberries, water, sugar, and stevia in a pan.
2. Bring to a boil over medium heat.
3. Cook, stirring often, until the cranberries start to pop.
4. Continue to cook and stir until most are popped and the sauce is the desired consistency.
5. After it is cooled, stir in the maple syrup, if using.

FRESH GARDEN TOMATO SALSA

*When your garden is overflowing with ripe tomatoes, make this fresh salsa.
I love it with those Beanitos chips! (It's best for eating right away
and not for use in recipes calling for salsa.)*

INGREDIENTS:

½ onion
4 cups coarsely chopped fresh tomatoes
1 (4-ounce) can green chilis
½ heaping teaspoon garlic powder
½ heaping teaspoon pepper
½ teaspoon salt

DIRECTIONS:

1. Place the onion in a large food processor and process until it is chopped into small pieces.
2. Add the tomatoes, chilis, garlic powder, pepper, and salt.
3. Pulse until well mixed, but not too long or the tomatoes will get too soupy.
4. Serve with chips.

SUGAR-FREE, DYE-FREE, NATURALLY FLAVORED REFRESHING DRINK

Don't feed your body those artificial colors and sweeteners, or gobs of sugar that are found in store-bought drinks. Make this instead. Your body will thank you.

INGREDIENTS:

6 cups water, divided
4 Black Cherry Berry tea bags
18 drops liquid stevia
2 cups ice
2 tablespoons apple cider vinegar

DIRECTIONS:

1. Bring 4 cups of the water to a boil.
2. Remove from heat and add the 4 tea bags.
3. Steep for 10 minutes.
4. Place ice in a glass pitcher.
5. Pour tea over the ice and let the ice melt.
6. Add the remaining 2 cups water and apple cider vinegar and stir.

MIX IT UP PARTY MIX

Gluten-free rice Chex and pretzels (Aldi's gluten-free pretzels are amazing!) are easy to come by these days, so go ahead and make your own party mix.

INGREDIENTS:

3 tablespoons grapeseed oil

1 tablespoon unsweetened almond or cashew butter

2 tablespoons coconut aminos

1 teaspoon coconut sugar

½ teaspoon garlic powder

½ teaspoon dried powdered mustard

½ teaspoon dried powdered ginger

4 cups gluten-free rice squares

2 cups gluten-free pretzels

DIRECTIONS:

1. Preheat oven to 250° F.
2. In a roasting pan, place the first 7 ingredients.
3. Place pan in the oven for 5 minutes.
4. Remove pan from the oven and stir in cereal and pretzels.
5. Bake for 30 minutes total, stirring every 10 minutes.
6. After 30 minutes, remove the pan from oven.
7. Cut open a paper grocery bag and lay flat.
8. Spread mix onto the paper bag to dry.
9. Store in an airtight container once the mix is thoroughly dry.

Made in the USA
Coppell, TX
17 December 2019